URBAN TALES OF THE BIBLE (PT 2)

BIBLE STORIES WITH A CONTEMPORARY "URBAN FLAIR"

JANUARY 17, 2022
Written by T.S. HOLDER

The Bible stories and version used in this publication were accessed, respectively, through https://www.biblegateway.com and "Scripture taken from *The Message*. Copyright © 1993, 1994, 1995, 1996, 2000, 2001, 2002. Used by permission of NavPress Publishing Group."

Printed in the United States of America

ISBN 9798-9854404-0-9

This series illuminates Biblical stories through the use of popular urban, true to life, language and humor, that presents Biblical stories in modern terms and with "**RAW**" facts <u>not often spoken from the **"politically correct" pulpit**</u>. The majority of the characters in the Bible are often portrayed as mindless individuals who go along and get along, and that never have an opinion or thought about what is going on what they are told to do, however in this series the silent Biblical characters are given a 'true-life' voice and their emotions are explored.

I dedicate this book to my deceased Father, "The Bishop" and to my deceased stepmother and friend, "Claudayshia", who unconditionally supported, loved and believed in me.

Part two picks up from the dramatic finale in part one with chapter 1 - "Jacob makes it to the East Sy-EEDE." Part two takes you on a round trip journey with Jacob, from arriving to the East Side, his explosive escapades with his uncle Laban and his journey home to face his brother Esau. There is so much in between that the best thing to do is to hang on to your braids, twists, weave and wigs.

If you are ready to start this next journey into Urban Tales of the Bible part two, all you gotta do is flip the page and let's get it!!

4

Table of Contents

Ch. 1 - Genesis 29 - Jacob makes it to the East Sy-eede!

Jacob was on his way! He had escaped the wrath of his brother Esau and moved on to new and different things. Jacob actually felt as though he was moving up since he was able to leave all of that inheritance drama behind and get away from his controlling ear hustlin' mama. Maybe now he could be his own man and not get caught up in his mother's sinister schemes. The way that Jacob is feeling now should take him to the top, but what will the future hold for Jacob. Is he truly his own man or is he still caught up in the family web and just doesn't know it yet?

This was all so exciting to Jacob, especially since he was always in the house, mostly the kitchen, while his brother Esau roamed freely about. He came to the land of the Eastern people. Yes, Jacob was now on the EAST SY-EEDE! Jacob felt as though he had finally made it! He stopped for a moment, looked around and just took it all in. What he was seeing was all so new to him and the culture of the Eastside people had him awestruck! We gotta remember that Jacob had lived a somewhat sheltered life and had not left his mother's house before. Yep, you got it, Jacob was a mama's boy! So can you imagine how he felt being in a new and different place out of the reach of his ear hustlin' mama? Jacob was all in.

As Jacob looked around he saw a watering well way, way out there in the distance of the country and it caught his eye. He saw three flocks of sheep lying near it and figured that the flocks must be watered from this well. He notice a large stone that was placed over the mouth of the well and thought to himself, "What in the world is that about?"

Later on Jacob noticed that when all the flocks were together at the well, all of the shepherds would physically roll the large stone away from the opening of the well so that they could water their sheep. The stone was so big that all of the shepherds worked together to roll it out of the way. After they finished giving their sheep water they would physically roll the large stone back over the opening of the well. Jacob thought to himself, "That seems pretty dangerous. That is a huge stone, seems like a brotha could get crushed if he wasn't careful."

Jacob was very curious about who these people were and what was up with that huge stone. The people looked very different than anyone that Jacob had ever seen. The way that they dressed and carried themselves seemed odd to Jacob and since he was all alone what he observed made him a bit fearful. Jacob shook the fear off and finally worked up the nerve to ask the shepherds at the watering hole a question. Jacob said, "Hey bruh! How ya doing? Could l ask where you from?"

One of the men answered and said, "Hey, what's up? No worries about asking us. We're all from Harran, ya know, the "Big H" and bruh, we can sure tell that you're not from around here."

Jacob wasn't just asking random questions to make conversation, he had a purpose in his questions. Jacob thought to himself, "Well this guy seemed to be pretty upfront and open to conversation. He didn't give me any static and I didn't sense a hostile attitude or unnecessary vibrato. I think I'll ask another question."

So once again Jacob worked up the courage and said, "Hey, by the way, do any of you know of or have any of you heard of Laban, Nahor's son?"

You see back then people were identified by their family. That's probably where southern folk get the saying, "Who ya people?"

This time all of the shepherds answered Jacob in one voice with a little harmony to the sound and said, "Yeah man, we know him! Everybody around here knows Laban!"

Jacob thought that he heard one of them mutter something like, "Yeah, we know him with his conniving self."

Jacob thought that was odd and said to himself, "Hmmm, that was an odd thing to say, but Laban is my mother's brother, so no tellin' what's up with him."

Then Jacob asked the men, "Do you know how he is doing? I mean he ain't sick or nothin', right?"

Once again they all answered in one voice and this time with a little bit of harmony and said, "He's doing alright as far as we know!"

This time you could hear a little bass, tenor, and alto, one of the men did a southern Baptist hum.

And just as they finished answering Jacob, one of them turned around and said, "Yo, dude! Look over there! Here comes Laban's daughter Rachel now. You see that fine young shorty with the sheep? Umm hmm, that's her. One thing about Laban, he maybe conniving, but he got ONE fine daughter! MMM Hmmm."

Jacob said, "Look, man, isn't it time for all of the animals to be gathered, so they can be watered and then taken back to the field?"

Jacob obviously wanted to speak with Rachel alone and not in front of the men, which is why he asked that question. In other words Jacob was saying, "Now you done served your purpose, don't you have some work to do, like water your sheep? That IS why you came here isn't it?"

All of the men replied to Jacob at the same time, "Man it ain't time to water no sheep! We can't water the sheep now. Just like we thought, you are most def not from around here!"

One of the men continued and said, "When all of US bring ALL of our sheep and we ALL gather HERE in this place in FRONT of THIS well, THEN and only THEN will we put our muscles together and roll that huge stone away from the opening of the well. THEN, we will water the sheep and take them back to pasture. We call it a pasture, not a field. Okay? You got it now?"

Remember, Esau worked with the animals and Jacob was in the kitchen so he had no earthly idea of how things worked outside of the house. He was a homebody that loved being in the kitchen making up new food dishes to try out on his greedy brother Esau. While they were still talking and explaining to Jacob, Rachel pulled up in her high end whip, with her father's sheep. Yes, Rachel knew her way around the field, I mean pasture. That was one shorty that knew how to handle the sheep just as well as the brothas did and this along with her being stunningly gorgeous gained her a lot of respect. Rachel was the Queen Bee of the Big H!!

CHILE, when Jacob laid his eyes on his "cousin" Rachel and all of the sheep she had, yes his cousin because she was daughter of his uncle Laban, Chile Jacob forgot all about what the men had just told him and HE went over to the well, all by himself, and pushed that stone away from the opening of the well and he watered his uncle's sheep! That was something to see! Jacob was just beside himself showing off and all! He then went over to Rachel and kissed her and as he kissed her HE started to cry. Yes, this grown man who had just shown up all of the other men by rolling the stone by himself began to cry like a baby who was still sucking his mama's breast.

I can only imagine what the other men were thinking. They didn't know whether to stomp Jacob for kissing Rachel or run because he had enough strength to roll the stone away by himself! They saw the brute force and strength that Jacob used while moving the stone by himself, but that didn't hold them back.

Facts: Jacob did not know Rachel when he kissed her and those men did not know Jacob, but yet and still they were ready to pimp slap him, however just as they were about to make a move Jacob started crying. One of the shepherds said to another, "Dude!! What's with him? First he pushed that huge stone away all by himself, trying to show off for Rachel, he kisses Rachel like he knows her and THEN him starts crying! What kinda foolishness is this? Who is this man child? I don't know if we should even consider runnin' up on him, he seems to be a little unstable, ya know, in the head!"

Jacob overheard the man and thought that he had better pull himself together and start splaining himself so he said to Rachel, "I hope that I didn't offend or scare you, but I am your cousin, on your father's side. My name is Jacob and my mother's name is Rebekah. She is your aunt, your father's sister. I know that your father, Laban, has told you stories about my mama?"

Gurl, when Rachel heard this, she left the sheep and her high end whip. Girlfriend ran to her daddy's house and told him what Jacob had said. She took off so fast, and didn't say anything to Jacob or the other men, Jacob really got scared then. He thought, "Oh Lawd, what have I done? She going to get her people. Ain't no tellin' what they gone do to me!"

Then Jacob started praying out loud and as he did the other men took a knee and joined him in prayer because they thought for sure he was a dead man standing. Jacob prayed. "Father God, in the name of Your son Jesus, who isn't even born yet and hasn't even been talked about yet, if it pleases You, I ask that You send Your angels to protect me from what is about to go down!"

And all the men said, "Amen! You got that right. Boy, that dude prayed a righteous prayer! Yeah he did!"

When Rachel finally reached her house she said, "Daddy, daddy! You won't buh-leeve it! You just won't believe it!"

Laban said, "What is going on? Why are you all hyped up like that? Did somebody mess with you?"

Rachel composed herself and said, "Just last night at dinner you were telling us a story about your sister Rebekah, and DADDY, lo and behold her son is at the well. He said that his name is Jacob and he is Aunt- tee Bekah's son! Come on now, we gotta get down to the well quickly, besides I was so excited that I ran off and left all of the sheep down there by themselves and my high end whip that you just bought me."

As soon as Rachel finished telling her father, he was ecstatic at the news about Jacob, his sister's son, HIS Nephew being in the area. Laban made a mad dash to the well to meet him. Once Laban finally got to the well and caught his breath, he grabbed Jacob and gave him a long hug and kissed him on the forehead. Laban grabbed Jacob and his things without saying a word and took him to his house with a quickness. Once they were there and Jacob was settled, they sat down and Jacob told Laban everything. Of course he didn't tell him how Esau wanted to kill him for stealing his blessing and inheritance, he skipped RIGHT over that part, but he did tell him the rest of the story.

Jacob's uncle Laban was so excited to see his family and his sister's son at that. He had not seen Rebekah or anyone from that side of the family since the last family funeral. We all know how that goes.

Laban said to Jacob, "WOW!! It's unbelievable that you are here. Man, finally, my own flesh and blood. Somebody who looks like my sister! WOW! It's unreal!"

Remember now that Jacob was on a mission to find a wife. Yes, he was running from what he had done to his brother, but his parents also told him to find a wife. So let's move the story ahead a little bit.

Now, Jacob had been at his uncle's place for about a month or so, working for his uncle for free. Sometimes family expects that from you especially when you come unannounced and stay for a long period of time. You know after a few days family is usually ready for you to leave and go on home. Eating up all of their food, sucking up the air conditioning and running up their bills. Laban was maybe a little different and he started feeling some kind of way about Jacob working for free, after all he wasn't broke or rich, but he definitely wasn't hurting for money, so he had a little meeting with Jacob and said, "Look young blood, just because we are family does not mean that you should work for me for free. I feel kinda bad about that, it just don't feel right deep down in my spirit. So, tell me how much do YOU think I should pay you? What do you think you and your skillz are worth? Speak up young blood, speak up! "

Before we get to Jacob's answer, let's look at something that's just laying around in the background waiting to be addressed. Laban had two daughters; the name of the older daughter was Leah, and the name of the younger daughter was Rachel. Leah was somewhat esthetically challenged,(she was ugly) the girl had weak eyes and wasn't as pretty as her sister Rachel, but Rachel, but RACHEL, had a lovely figure and was gorgeous. Jacob was a witness to that and he started checkin' for Rachel the moment he saw her. Why else do you think he pushed that huge stone from the well by himself and watered the sheep that Rachel was supposed to water? If that is not enough proof, bruh kissed her at the well and didn't even know her name. Yes, Jacob fell hard and quick for Rachel!! His nose was wide open and he was in love with Rachel at first sight. Jacob was so in love that when his uncle asked him the question about his pay Jacob thought it was the perfect opportunity to make his intentions known!! Jacob finally replied to his uncle

Laban, "I'll work for you for seven years for free, just as long as at the end of those seven years I can be with Rachel, your YOUNGER daughter, my YOUNGEST cousin RACHEL."

Notice here that Jacob specified, your younger daughter, my youngest cousin RACHEL. He wanted to be sure that there was no misunderstanding about why he was working so hard and what he expected at the end of those seven years. He didn't want to get stuck with Leah. He had only been there a month or so but he noticed that Laban never sent Leah with the sheep, he only ever sent Rachel out into the public eye. He was trying to get Rachel noticed by the other shepherds, but he kept Leah in the background because of her weak eyes. We all know that weak eyes meant that her ugliness made your eyes weak to look at her!

If Jacob had been thinking about his uncle's question and him feeling bad about Jacob working for free for him, he could have asked for Rachel right then and there since he had been working for free. She could have been back pay so to speak, but that shows how precious Rachel was to Jacob. A man that offers to work seven years for free for a woman to become his wife is truly in love. You gotta think, Jacob didn't have a desk job or a kitchen job, he was in for some serious physical labor. Jacob was used to working in the kitchen when he was at home with mom and dad, so his body had some adjusting to do and he had a lot to learn.

After Laban heard Jacob's offer, he tried to play it off and said, "Well, I guess it would be better that I give her to you and keep her in the family. Alright, alright, that

15

sounds like a plan young blood. Work for me for FREE for SEVEN years and Rachel is all yours."

So with the deal being made, Jacob worked seven HARD years and did his job with perfection, because he thought that he would be getting perfection when he finally got Rachel. To Jacob those seven years seemed like only a few days because he was head over heels for Rachel. Bruh's nose was "Mack-truck" wide open. But it is apparent that Jacob forgot all about what the men at the well said. Remember one of them muttered under his breath that Laban was conniving? Let's see if it's true or not.

After seven years Jacob went to his uncle and said, "Alright then unc, it's time for you to give me my wifey, my bae, Rachel. I did my seven years with style and I want my bae Rachel. It's time that I am able to show Rachel just how much I love her."

Here it is!! Ups jump the devil! Laban was just like his scheming ear hustlin sister Rebekah. He had been plotting, planning, scheming and preparing for this day. He had the last seven years to put this game plan together. Laban thought that since Jacob loved Rachel so much he would use this to his advantage. So he had a big house party in Jacob's honor and invited all the people in the Big H to come. He had food, wine and music everywhere! That house party was talked about months after it was over. After the party ended and it was time for Jacob to be with Rachel Laban thought to himself, "Let the games begin! Camera, set, action."

Laban gave his maid Zilpah to Leah as her assistant and said to Leah, "Now daughter I want you to go and sneak into that tent with Jacob and take your sister's place."

Leah replied, "Uh, no daddy no!! How dare you ask me to do that! I can't do that to my baby sister. She is crazy over Jacob! Why in the world would you ask me to do something like this? Are you for real right now?!"

Laban replied, "Gurl, if you don't get yo crack in that tent! Now you know that this is about the only way I am going to get you a man and marry you off. No man that has seen you in the light of day, or any other light for that matter, has offered to marry you since we've been here. NO ONE HAS BEEN CHECKIN' FOR YOU!! You KNOW that every man here in the East has seen you and not one of them has asked to even go out with you, so this is your one and only chance to get a husband. Gurl, hurry up and get yo crack in that tent with that man and make sure that the lights stay off until morning."

If this doesn't sound just like that same mess Rebekah pulled on Isaac and Esau! Messiness must run in the family! Once Leah was in the tent and since Jacob had never been with Rachel before he didn't know the difference in their bodies, so Jacob proceeded to get down to grown folks business with whom he THOUGHT was the one he loved. That tent was rocking that night as Jacob pulled out all of the stops that he had been rehearsing in his mind to let Rachel know just how much he loved her. BUT WHEN MORNING CAME, oh Lord, it hit the fan and all bets were off!!

Jacob rolled over and opened his eyes to behold Rachel's beauty in the morning light and the man screamed, yes chile, he actually screamed! Rumor has it that Jacob ran out of that tent like something was chasing him. The look on his face was like he was petrified. He came flying out of that tent with a quickness and did the 100 yard dash to get to his uncle Laban.

While he was running to find his uncle he thought about the trick that he and his mother had pulled on Isaac and Esau and how this must be punishment and payback. When Jacob finally found his uncle Laban he said, "You are truly my mother's brother. This is the same kind of mess that she pulled on my father and my brother. Her foolishness is why I had to come here with you! What have you done to me? How could you do this to me after how hard I worked for you and for free? I thought that we were better than this! You are just like my mother! If you weren't my uncle, I'd beat you within an inch of your life! I served you for Rachel, not lazy eyed, ugly and can't get a man LEAH! WHY?"

We know by now that uncle Laban is quick to run game and has a slick mouth, so he replied, "Young blood!! Young blood calm down! You gotta know how we do things around here! No one gives the baby girl away before the older one is married. Come on now, you really expected me to break custom for you! I knew that you showed up on my doorstep outta nowhere because you were running from something. I know my sister Rebekah and you did not just come here for a visit! And why in the world would you think that seven years is enough for my beautiful baby girl? Do you know how many of these shepherds have made me offers for Rachel, and since you came on the scene the offers have been pouring in? Dude, anyone can see how you two have been checkin' for each other since you got here. It is not our custom to give the baby girl before the older one is married. Now go and enjoy your honeymoon with Leah and because you still want Rachel, if you work another seven years for free, I will give you Rachel. Now get out of my face and go enjoy my beautiful, well go enjoy my daughter!"

Jacob left, but believe me when I tell you he was 38 hot and wanted to do his uncle. All the way back to the tent he thought about how he had lost Rachel and how could he trust his uncle to do the right thing after another seven years. More importantly he did not think that Rachel would want him after he had been with her sister. That's like breaking a sister code! But because he loved Rachel so much he forced himself to spend the honeymoon week with Leah and because he did, his uncle Laban felt bad (as he should have) about the boy being with ugly Leah and surprised Jacob with Rachel right after the honeymoon week was over! Laban surprised Rachel and gave her his servant Bilhah as her assistant. Either unc was feeling generous or feeling bad about the stunt he pulled on his two daughters and his nephew.

If you thought that the tent was rocking when Jacob was with Leah, you gotta know that Jacob sent Leah out for a night with the girls while he made the tent romantic for Rachel. Jacob had rose petals all over the tent floor and bed, he had scented amber candles burning, the hot tub was ready and of course some red wine. Jacob made serious love to Rachel that night. He had held back a few tricks when he was with Leah, thinking that he would need to keep them for later, but this time he held nothing back.

After the honeymoon with Rachel, Jacob found that having his true love by his side made the next seven years go by faster than the first seven years.

Because Jacob loved Rachel so much, he did not pay much attention to Leah. It was so obvious that even GOD noticed Leah being alone and feeling unloved. Leah's father Laban was so glad that she was off of his hands that he hardly paid any attention to her or what was going on with her and Jacob. Jacob had his lover Rachel and focused all of his attention on her, so poor Leah was left all alone and by herself. She would often use the dry begging technique on Jacob to get him to be with her, but it didn't work! The Lord had mercy on Leah and Jacob decided to give Leah her once a month "just because we married" sex. That is similar to the social security or disability check that comes once a month, just enough to get you by until the next check comes. So Leah had her once a month intimacy with Jacob. It was just enough to keep her out of his hair, but when Jacob did sleep with her, she became pregnant. Now this made Rachel feel some kind of way towards Leah. Rachel thought to herself, "First she steals my man and now she is pregnant by him before I am?"

Leah had a son! She gave Jacob his first heir and she named him Reuben and said, "I have had this baby boy because the Lord saw how miserable and lonely I was. After having Jacob's first son even before Rachel, I feel more than positive that he will love me more than Rachel now! He has to! After all he was my husband first."

The Lord really had mercy on her and heard her cries because when Jacob came back around again to give Leah her monthly lovin' she got pregnant again!! This time around she had another son for Jacob and named him Simeon and said, "The Lord really does have my back He gave me another son to love since Jacob still actin' funny and things!"

By this time Rachel was off her chain, because she was still not able to give her true love a son. She just couldn't understand it because Jacob was with her more than with Leah.

Jacob slept with Leah again and wouldn't you know it, oh girl got pregnant again! She had another son! She named this one Levi and said, "The count is now my three sons to Rachel's big zero!! Prayerfully and hopefully since Jacob now has three sons by me he will fall in love with me!"

Apparently Jacob wasn't getting the message about showing Leah more love so the Lord took pity on Leah again. This time Jacob slept with her and she got pregnant a fourth time. This time she had another son and named him Judah and said, "You know what, the Lord is showing me how much HE loves me and Jacob is STILL not showing me the love that I deserve, so guess what, this time I am going to be thankful to the Lord and praise Him for my four sons! I am going to show God all of my love, He'll appreciate it more!"

It seems that Jacob wasn't the only one that the Lord had a message for because when Leah had her fourth son and thanked and praised the Lord, she didn't have any more children at all for Jacob. It seems that Leah's message was to lean on God and He will see her through this nightmare of a marriage.

How do you think that Rachel is feeling about her sister having all of these children and she does not have one as of yet and she and Jacob have been putting in time in the bedroom more than he and Leah? Is Rachel about to get in her feelings and go off or does she have a plan to remedy the situation like Sarah did with her husband Abraham?

Pont to Ponder: When Laban pulled a fast one on Jacob by sending Leah into his tent instead of Rachel, was this Jacob's punishment for the trick that he and his mother Rebekah pulled on Esau and Isaac? Remember Jacob went into his father's tent and pretended to be Esau? Hmm?

Take Away: When we have interactions with people, regardless of if they are family or not, be sure to deal with whoever it is in all honesty and truth. We see from what happened to Jacob having to leave home and then coming to his Uncle Laban's in a deceitful manner, that these things will catch up with you when you least expect it. So in order to avoid having to look over your shoulder or worry about when the hammer will fall just be upfront and transparent.

Prayer: Father we thank You today that You are giving us the ability to do and say what is right and to always be honest and transparent in all that we do. Show us how to treat others as we ourselves would want to be treated.

Ch. 2 – Genesis 30 - Cousin Wife, Rachel still ain't pregnant!

Jacob had been spending almost every night with his bae Rachel and tried his best to get her pregnant. He was spending so much time with her, not only because he was in love with her, but because he could see just how much she was hurting from seeing her sister Leah, whom Jacob was tricked into marrying, having four sons by Jacob when she hadn't even given him one. Cousin wife Rachel was over the top in her emotions and felt that she had to do something or she might lose Jacob to Leah.

The biggest portion of Rachel's emotions were jealousy and anger. She was jealous because her ugly sister Leah was pushing out babies like there was no tomorrow and she was angry because she couldn't understand why this was happening to her. She had always been the obedient daughter. She never once even looked at any of the shepherds, and that was the truth because she was a virgin when she slept with Jacob.

Rachel had heard a story about Rebekah's mother-in-law named Sarah and so the story is told, Sarah had the same problem. Sarah was unable to give her husband Abraham a son, so she took matters into her own hands and gave her husband permission to marry and sleep with her servant Hagar. She had also heard how Hagar gave Abraham a son. Rachel knew of the problems that this caused between Abraham and Sarah and how Abraham had to send the side chick and her son away because she was trying to step all over Sarah, but Rachel thought that she and Jacob were too close to let anything like that happen. Did Rachel really think this all the way through? Just like Sarah, it seems that Rachel did not take everything and everyone involved into consideration.

Rachel came up with a plan to make this happen. The first part of the plan was to manipulate Jacob by using reverse psychology to make him go along with whatever she said. Rachel waited gooood until Jacob came in from the fields, washed up, ate and was ready to spend some intimate time with her. She had even prepared his favorite meal to set the stage. Then Rachel hit him below the belt and said, "Why can't you get me pregnant so that I too can give you a son? I feel like I am dying over here waiting for you to do your duties as a husband!! Is there something wrong with me or maybe it's you? Am I working with a man that has damaged goods?"

That was some low down dirty below the belt messy words that Rachel spoke to her cousin husband, Jacob. Jacob was within his rights to go left and he did! Jacob said, "Why are you blaming me?! We can both see how many sons your sister Leah has given me and YOU, you haven't even given me one, but you want to sit there and say that something is wrong with ME!! Gurl! Gurl, I give my best loving to you! You betta go somewhere with all of that! I'm gonna keep it a buck with you, you betta get on your knees and ask God what's up, because only God can say who will have a baby and who will not! The only thing that I need to do is to keep loving you as much as I can!"

Rachel thought about what he said and thought to herself, "Oh yeah, the plan is most certainly working as I thought it would. He's all mad now, so let me just keep this going!"

Rachel said to Jacob, "What if I give you my maid, Bilhah? Ya know, the one that my father gave me to come here with me when I married you? What if I give her to you so that you can make love to her, and she can carry the baby for me? This way we can have a son together and start OUR family, OUR FAMILY, separate from Leah."

Now just like Abraham, Jacob is a man and of course he didn't turn the offer down. Jacob slept with the maid, and of course, she got pregnant and had a boy!

Rachel was overjoyed that Bilhah had a baby boy for her husband Jacob. She said to herself, "God has truly heard my prayers and gave me the breakthrough that I needed to gain my dignity back!"

Rachel named the baby Dan, which means vindication. Rachel thought that baby boy Dan had taken away the stain of her not being able to get pregnant for her husband, but is that truly the case?!

Rachel thought that things were going pretty good and maybe she could catch up with her sister Leah and pass her. Rachel wanted to have more baby boys than Leah, so she told Jacob to sleep with Bilhah again and guess what, Bilhah got pregnant again and had another boy. Rachel was over the top again with joy. She thought to herself, "I knew that this would work and me and Jacob would stay solid and drama free."

Rachel said, "I am going to name this son Naphtali!! I am naming him this because Leah and I have been going at it ever since she stole my husband and started having sons for him, but this time I have won the fight!"

I guess that Rachel thought that Leah was going to remain silent and allow her to do what she was doing without coming back at her. Oh but no!! Leah had more fight in her than Rachel realized. Leah said, "Who in the world does that heifer think she is?! Jacob and I were just fine until she came into the tent! I see that Bilhah only had two sons for Jacob and since the second one, nothing else has happened!! It's obvious to me that the Lord will not give me more children, so I am going to do like my sister did, I am going to give my maid to Jacob to sleep with. I already know that Jacob won't say no and being the type of man that he is, he will go along with it. I have seen him looking at her, checking her out. I guess he figures that he might as well spread himself around. After all it is his household."

Leah talked to Jacob and said, "Looks like Rachel's maid has stopped giving you sons, Rachel still can't have any and neither can I. You do want more, right?"

Jacob said, "Yes, I would like as many as possible. Why are you asking me this? You already know!"

Leah said, "What if I do the same thing that Rachel did? What if I give you my maid, Zilpah, as your wife, to make love to? I know that she will be able to give you another son."

Of course we know that Jacob agreed, with his greedy self. So Jacob slept with Zilpah, his third wife, and she got pregnant and they had a baby boy. Leah was so happy and felt blessed so she named the baby Gad.

Leah thought to herself, "This is going really well, I think I will tell Jacob to sleep with her again. After all I did give her to him as his wife, unlike my sister Rachel, she gave her maid Bilhah to Jacob as a side chick."

So Jacob slept with Zilpah again and again she had another boy. Leah was overjoyed and started singing and rapping, "Uh-huh, uh-huh, I got it, I got it!"

Leah thought to herself, "All the women in the camp will look up to me and bring gifts to me and my son. This will not only make me happy, but Jacob will be happy too."

So Leah name this baby boy Asher, which means happy.

Remember Jacob and Leah's first son named Reuben, well he is old enough now to roam about outside. It was during the time of year when the servants gather the crops and bring them in just before winter hits. Reuben was outside playing and found some pretty flowers that were white and purple and had large yellow berries on them. Reuben had not seen anything like this before. He picked one up and looked at it and thought that the root of it was shaped almost like a person. Reuben said, "I gotta take this to mama. I don't know what this is, but I know that she will know."

Reuben was on his way to the tent to take the flower to his mama and on the way he saw his aunt Rachel and waved at her with the plant in his hand. Rachel looked astonished and shocked and walked right behind him.

Reuben gave it to his mother and asked, "Mama, what is this? It looks so pretty on top but like a person on the bottom."

Leah said, "Son, it is called Mandrake root."

Reuben said, "Why does it look so different than the other plants?"

Leah Said, "Well son, it is supposed to help a woman get pregnant and have a child. Woman search day and night looking for these and if they find them they usually sell them for lots of money to women who do not have children, ya know, somebody like your aunt Rachel."

Reuben said, "Okay mama."

And with that Reuben went back outside to play. As soon as he left the tent in pops Rachel with her ear hustling self. She was standing outside the tent listening to the conversation and found out that she was right, Reuben did have a mandrake.

Rachel came on in to the tent with a boldness and said to Leah, "I saw Reuben walking with something in his hand that looked like a Mandrake root? Is that it over there?"

Leah gave Rachel the side eye and said, "Yeah! What about it?"

Rachel said, "Well you see, you know that I have not been able to get pregnant?"

Leah interrupted and said, "That part! Me and everyone else knows that you have not been able to get pregnant by Jacob who gets everyone else pregnant! What's your point?"

Normally Rachel and Leah would have been going at it, but since Leah had something that Rachel wanted, Rachel humbled herself, overlooked the slick mouth remarks and continued by saying, "AND God knows that Jacob and I been tryin' hard gurl! So do you think that I can have just a little bit of the mandrake root so that I can give Jacob a son?"

Leah thought to herself, "This heifer comes in here asking for my son's mandrake so that she can give my husband a baby! Who in the world does she think she is or better yet, who in the world does she think I am?"

Leah tore into Rachel and said, "Heifer, you got some nerve!! You have never even apologized for stealing my husband and now you think that I am going to give you some of my sons mandrake so that YOU can have a baby with MY husband. Gurl, you got me twisted!"

Rachel, being the crafty one that she is, thought to herself, "I know that she wants to be with Jacob and he hasn't touched her in a long time so I am going to use that to my advantage."

Rachel said to Leah, "Ok, I admit that you are right, well almost right. Jacob and I were supposed to get married before you and you and daddy tricked him and me. That is not my fault. However back to the matter at hand. What if I told Jacob to sleep with you tonight? Wouldn't that be a good exchange for some of the mandrake root?"

Leah was like, "Gurl say no more. How much do you want?"

All that Leah wanted was to be loved by Jacob just as he loved Rachel. So as soon as Jacob walked into the tent from working Leah was all over him like black on beauty.

Jacob was like, "Hold up, hold up! What are you doing? It is not your turn until I say it is your turn."

Leah said, "Rachel said that it was okay. She traded you for some of Reuben's mandrake roots. I will take you however I can get you! Come on and let me love on you tonight."

Jacob, with his weak self, went on into the other tent with Leah and they got down to grown folks business that night! Lord have mercy and would you not know it, um huh that's right, Leah got pregnant again and had a fifth son for Jacob!! This time Leah named the baby Issachar and thought the weirdest thing to herself, "God saw me give my maid Zilpah to my husband Jacob as his wife and God thought that was good and he gave me another son!"

How did Leah come to that conclusion? Anywho, Leah offered Rachel some more of the mandrake root in exchange for her having another night with Jacob. Rachel agreed without any discussion. So Jacob and Leah slept together again and old fertile Leah got pregnant again! Chile that's numero 6 for Leah and Jacob AND it was another boy. She named this one Zebulun which means honor. What a name!

Anywho, Leah thought to herself, "Surely God has heard ME because I have given Jacob six baby boys and Rachel hasn't given him any, still not yet, even with the mandrake! LOL!! SMH. I know that I am the one that the Lord wants to be Jacob's true wife, not Rachel or any of the others. Maybe Jacob will bring me something special for giving him six boys."

Now Leah became greedy and wanted to be with Jacob again. Of course we all know how Jacob feels about this, so he slept with Leah again, and yes history repeated itself, Leah got pregnant again!! HOWEVER, this time she did not have a boy, oh girl had a girl! Leah named her Dinah. Dinah is the only girl so far and she has many big brothers, so she will be well protected or will she?

Rachel was feeling some kind of way because Jacob kept sleeping with Leah and Leah kept having babies and boys at that! When Leah had the girl, Rachel rushed over to Jacob and said, "Ok mister man, your time with Leah is up!! It is time for you to bring yourself on home to me, your one and only!!"

Jacob had great stamina and strength, but was so weak when it came to women. So of course Jacob slept with Rachel and OMG, Rachel finally got pregnant. Chile the entire camp was singing praises to Rachel saying, "This time she did it! Oh gur-url finally did it!"

Rachel felt so good about herself and thought, "God has finally heard my prayers and let me give my man a boy!! There's no more shame holding me. I am blessed! I am finally like the other women and Jacob my husband, my baby daddy will no longer feel sorry for me."

Rachel named the baby boy Joseph and asked the Lord, "Please give me more baby boys to make Jacob happy?"

Besides all of that drama, Jacob was tired of working for his slick conniving uncle Laban. Jacob's 14 years of labor were over and he wanted to go back home, even though his mother Rebekah had not sent anyone to say that Esau had calmed down and it was safe to come back. Jacob thought that after 14 years Esau should have finally cooled down and hopefully forgot about it. Jacob did not care one way or the other because he had had enough of Laban and wanted his own space and place to raise his family.

Jacob said to Laban, "Yo, Unc! I have many sons and one daughter. I have wives and I need to go back home so that I can be around my people, have my own place and enough space to raise my family. I am asking you to pay me what I have worked for, let me take my wives and children and be on my way! I need to get outta here. Besides the women are so cramped for space that they are going after each other to see who can have the most sons for me and they are wearing me out!"

Laban was kind of expecting this to happen because he knew his daughters. Laban said, "Nephew, calm down. I understand. Also I was going to talk with you an-ty-ways because word on the street is that because of you and your work I have been blessed and have increased, so name your price!"

Jacob said, "Now unc, you know exactly what I have done for you. When I came here you only had the few sheep that Rachel took to the well to water. You weren't rich and you weren't poor, you hardly had anything at all, but now because of my hard work and how I cared for the livestock with perfection you have so much more! You are not fair to midland wealthy anymore, but have become rich off of my back. I know that it is time for me to leave here and do the same for my family, wouldn't you agree?"

Jacob continued, "You asked me what you should pay me? To start with and so that you can see just how much I have done for you, let me take all of the sheep and goats that are speckled or spotted and that are dark in color and that will be my payment. Also, you can use this method to check my level of honesty and integrity to you. So when you come to check my flocks if you find any sheep or goat that is not spotted, speckled or dark in color than you will know that I stole it from you."

Laban said, "You know what nephew, young blood that sounds like a fair plan. I will have my men to take only the white sheep and goats for me and the spotted, speckled and dark ones are yours. I will also have my men to take my sheep at least 3 days away from you and yours so that they do not get mixed up again."

Jacob said, "That's what's up! Bet that. Sounds great unc, let's do this thang."

Laban thought that his part of the sheep and goats would be much, much more than Jacob's. He thought that he had the best end of the deal.

 Jacob thought to himself, "I gotta do something to take care of my family. Unc has the best of the herd and the most, but I will figure something out."

Jacob, was a smart man and had learned a lot since he was away from his mother's kitchen. Jacob thought to himself, "Well if I can use certain items in the kitchen to make the food look a certain color let me see if it will work on the herd."

So Jacob took some fresh branches from three types of trees, the poplar tree, the almond tree and the plane tree. Jacob took his pocket knife and took the bark off of several small tree branches. Jacob wanted all of the darkness to be gone. He used the branches like the women were using the mandrake roots.

Jacob placed the small white tree branches from all three of the trees right where the sheep came to drink water. He wanted the sheep to be able to look at the branches while they were drinking. So the story is told that when the animals were ready to have sex with one another and were thirsty, the sheep went to where the water was, drank the water and had sex in front of the water which had the white branches. This caused the herd to have baby animals that were streaked spotted and speckled.

That wasn't all that Jacob did. I told you he was a smart man! He took the young animals that had just been born spotted and speckled and placed them in an area by themselves. Then he took the others that had been around for a while and had them to look at Laban's animals. So Jacob had the stronger animals of the flock and did not mix them with the weak animals that Laban had. So whenever the strong female animals wanted to mate with the male animals he would place the white branches in the watering area and so with this Jacob was growing a large herd of animals for himself and he could better provide for and take care of his family.

Jacob's flock grew and grew. He had huge flocks of animals that included sheep, goats, camels and donkeys. Jacob also had to hire male and female servants to help him out because he had so many animals that it was way too much for him to handle alone.

How do you think that Uncle Laban is going to feel about Jacob growing so much, especially when he thought that he had the larger amount of animals?

36

Point to Ponder: Why couldn't Rachel have children like her sister Leah, especially since Jacob was her man to start with? Shouldn't it have been Leah that couldn't have babies, since she stole Rachel's husband? Why were both Rachel and Leah so quick to give their female maids to their husband to have sex and babies with?

Take Away: Jacob's family and animals were increasing in numbers, far beyond what he imagined. Even when the odds are stacked against us and we have less than we should, God can give us the formula to increase and multiply just as he did Jacob.

Prayer: Father we thank You today for bringing increase into our lives. We thank You that You are giving us ideas and inventions that will bring financial increase not only for us but for our family members as well.

Ch. 3 – Genesis 31 - Jacob bounces and gets the heck away from Unc!

Jacob was in the fields working hard. Making sure that his animals were being taken care of because he knew that these animals were God's resource of wealth to him and that they would make it possible for him to take care of his family once he left his uncles' house.

While Jacob was in the field he overheard some of his cousins talking smack about him. When Jacob would see them around the way and speak they would just give him the side eye and keep it movin'. His cousins wouldn't say anything to his face but the minute Jacob's back was turned they carried on scandalously! They would say things like, "Man, who does Jacob think he is? He came here out of nowhere, married both of our sisters and now he has taken all of our father's money making animals. That was OUR inheritance that he has taken! We gotta find a way to put an end to this or we won't have anything!"

Another could be heard saying, "Yeah he did, and you know what? Jacob used to be humble and respectful, but now he has let all of our father's wealth go to that ole big head of his. Just look at how he walks around here, look at him! Like he owns the block or something!"

Keep in mind that Jacob had not changed. Jacob had always been upfront with his uncle, well except when he first came there when he didn't tell them why he was running from his hometown, but otherwise he had been truthful, humble and respectful of who he was and where he was. It's funny how wealth changes the eyesight of those who feel as though all of the money should be in their possession.

Jacob also noticed that his Uncle Laban was acting some kind of way towards him. He wasn't the same cheerful, joking uncle that he was when Jacob first arrived. Jacob tried to pin it down to when unc started changing and as he thought about it he remembered unc's attitude started changing towards him when they divided the sheep. It was almost as if Laban was avoiding him and was doing something behind Jacob's back.

It was at this moment that Jacob fell to his knees and said, "Lord, now you know my heart and you KNOW that I have done nothing but be fair and honest since I have been here, what is the problem with my uncle and cousins? Why are they living in their feelings and taking it out on me? Please show me what is up with my people. I am asking You to expose their inner feelings towards me and put them on blast for all to see. Lord please vindicate me."

The Lord answered and said, "Jacob it's very simple! Your time here is up! You have worn out your welcome and it is time to go back to your mom and dad's. Go back to your own hometown away from these people. Pack up your family and all that you own and go. I will be with you as you take the long trip back. I got you!"

After Jacob had prayed and talked with the Lord about the sichimation, he had one of his servants to go and bring Leah and Rachel out to the field where he was so that he could talk with them. Jacob was expecting them to be there right away, but for some odd reason the women thought that Jacob wanted to have a lunch date with them. They both tried to prepare a lunch better than the other so it was like a couple of hours had passed before they came to the field where Jacob was. When they got there Jacob said, "Good God! What the heck took so long? I know you were told I wanted to see you right away and that it's urgent? Good thing I wasn't laying here having a heart attack or something! I'd be dead and gone to glory waiting on you two!"

Leah said, "Well, I thought it was a lunch date so I prepared you a fabulous lunch filled with your favorite foods. I would have been done much sooner, but RACHEL kept getting in my way. I told her to go SAT DOWN somewhere but as usual she wouldn't listen. You and I both know that she can't cook anyways. Girlfriend can't even boil hot water!"

Rachel said, "I know you didn't! Stop trying to blame everything on me. As soon as the servant came I grabbed some leftovers, heated them and packed them up. I was ready in under 10 minutes, the rest of the time was spent waiting on your slow mo behind. You know if we weren't in public right now, gurl you just don't know!! I just can't with you right now, but you just wait! Watch yo back gurl, watch yo back!"

Jacob said, "Alright, alright enough of this. For y'all to be sisters you act more like rival street gang members. Look, what I wanted to talk to you about is this, have either of you noticed how cold your father has been acting? He's been acting some kind of way when it comes to me. He doesn't have anything to say to me anymore, but your brothers have a lot to say about me behind my back. They are trying to say that I stole your father's animals and wealth. That I am taking their inheritance. You know that I have only been fair and honest towards your father and have worked like a slave for him.

Regardless of what I do, your father runs game on me like I am supposed to be stupid and don't know what he's doing, but I let it slide because he is your father. He takes money out of my checks for no reason, talkin' bout inflation! But you know there is one thing that I can say, the more your father mistreats and cheats me, the more God blesses me. If your father wants all of the white animals, usually because there are more, then God blesses my flocks to increase with speckled, spotted and dark animals. Then your father will see more speckled, spotted and dark so he will want those and give me the white ones and then the white ones increase. There is no pleasing him, because he wants it all and wants me to have nothing. Each time your father acts a fool, God takes that foolishness and increases me. God spoke to me in a dream and said, 'Jacob, don't think that I don't know what Laban is doing to you because I know exactly what he is trying to do. Each time he tries to take what I am giving you, I give you more!! I want you to leave from your uncle's place because he is a crooked, self-serving, scheming and conniving shyster. He only thinks of himself. You need to go back to your hometown right now. Laban is coming for you every chance he gets!"

Rachel and Leah agreed with Jacob and both of them said, "We know exactly what you are talking about. He treats us the same way. It's as if after we married you, we were no longer his daughters. He looks at us as if he never knew us. We both know that he has always been money hungry and all that he wanted was to sell us to the first man that had good money so that he could go on a wild spending spree, buying junk. Look at this place, he is turning into a hoarder! The one thing that we both agree on is that we are going to take what we can from daddy since he wants to act like that. It's our payment for how he now treats us. So bay-bay, you do what you gotta do and we got your back!"

The next day, Jacob woke up real early with a new attitude and his hometown on his mind. The night before the ladies and staff had very quietly packed things up so that no one would know what was going on. Jacob made sure that he had all of his livestock and everything that he owned. He had the ladies wake the kids and place them on the camels and donkeys and then everyone was ready to go.

Just before they pulled out, Rachel said, "Wait a minute I think I left something. I want to do one more quick looksee to be sure."

Jacob said, "Okay, but make it quick because we need to leave before your father comes back from shaving the wool off the sheep. I don't want to get into it with him, because at this point I won't be so respectful."

Rachel said, "Okay, I'll be right back."

Rachel hurried off, but she went around the back side of the tent so that no one could see her. She ran into her father's house and took the gods that her father worshipped. She remembered each place in the house that her father kept the idols. Rachel grabbed them and as she was running back to the camel she thought to herself, "This will teach the old buzzard. Now he will know just how me and Leah feel about how he has treated us and our children. Serves him right!"

As she was getting on the camel everyone in the caravan, even the children said, "Geeesh, it's about time. What took you so long? Thought you said you'd be right back? And then you didn't even bring anything back with you. Did you have to use the bathroom one last time or something?"

Jacob said, "Alright enough! Rachel get on your camel and let's ride out!"

Laban and none of his people had any idea of what was going on. By the time news from the street reached Laban and he figured out what had taken place it was 72 hours later. Jacob was long gone by then. Before they pulled out Jacob told everyone that they were not stopping to any restaurants to eat and there would be one bathroom and rest stop per day and that would be when he stopped to fill up the camels and donkeys.

It was all over the Live at Five morning news. The news reporter said that there had been reports of a massive caravan of people and animals spotted on the way out of the Big H. The reports had started coming into law enforcement authorities before the break of day. It seems that as quiet as Jacob and his people thought they were, they were not!! With all of the animals walking at a fast pace and dust flying Jacob should have known that someone would hear them and report the disturbance. Once the news reached Laban, it is said that Laban issued an Amber, Silver and Green alert. If you knew Laban you would know that the Green alert stood for "Somebody stole my money." Laban got his crew together with a quickness, so that he could pull up on Jacob and his daughters. The word on the street is that a week later Laban and his men finally caught up with Jacob in the hill country near Gilead. However, before Laban actually reached Jacob the Lord spoke to him in a dream and warned Laban by saying, "When you reach Jacob and your daughters, be careful, be very careful how you handle and treat them. You treat Jacob with respect and honor. I am warning you, don't go over there acting like your usual crazy self!"

When Laban finally got there, Jacob had set up tents to rest for the night, so Laban rolled up on Jacob and had his people to set up his tents right next to Jacob.

Laban ran over to Jacob's tent and went slap off on Jacob, "Young blood! Nephew! What's up with you sneaking off like a thief in the night? Why did you feel like you had to run off like that? You didn't even give me a chance to say goodbye to my daughters and grandchildren! What's going on in that little mind of yours?"

Jacob said, "We both know how you have been acting towards me and your daughters. You treated us like we were from the wrong side of the hood, so we figured that you wouldn't miss us. We figured that you wouldn't want to say goodbye especially since you couldn't even say good morning when we were there. You treated us like you wanted us out of your life."

Laban came back strong, "You took my daughters in the dark of night and ran off like you stole something! Did you steal something? You know that I would have had a big house party to send you all off in style. I would have had a live old school band, plenty of food and an open bar, but naw, you ran off and took that away from me."

Laban continued, "I came here with a mind to crush you like an ant! I have the power to do that you know. The only reason that you are still standing is because Isaac's God spoke to me in a dream and told me not to hurt you and to be careful how I handle you."

Laban walked around, back and forth and said, "I am sure that after 14+ years of being away from your family that you probably want to see your parents and your

44

hometown. I get that, however what I don't get is why you had to steal my house gods. My idols?"

Jacob said, "I left so suddenly because of the way you had been acting, the way your sons were acting and talking, so I was scared of what might happen if I stayed any longer. I felt like I had worn out my welcome. As far as your house gods and idols I don't know anything about that and I don't know what to tell you."

Jacob felt confident that no one had Laban's gods but what he didn't know is that Rachel was not looking around or using the bathroom one last time, but she was being roguish and stealing from her father so Jacob said, "Go ahead and search everything that we have and if by chance you do find your gods, whoever has them will be deaded."

Upon hearing this and getting the go ahead from Jacob, Laban started his search. All the time that he is going from tent to tent he was saying to himself, "I am not sure why Jacob wants to play games with me. You gotta get up pretty early in the morning to get the drop on me. I know that I will find my gods here in one of their tents. If I had an extra god I would put it in one of these tents, set Jacob up and take everything that he has. After all it's all mine anyways!!"

The first place that Laban looked of course was in Jacob's tent since he was the head of everything. Of course Laban found nothing. He proceeded to Leah's tent and thought to himself, "I don't know why I am looking in here she doesn't have the strength or brains to do anything like this."

45

Laban found nothing in Leah's tent, so he proceeded to the tents of the other women and finally Rachel's tent. Laban found nothing in any of the women's tents except bras, panties and other feminine items.

Unknown to Jacob or anyone else Rachel had placed her father's idols in her saddle bag that was on the camel she was riding. When Laban came towards Rachel as if he were going to search her saddle bag Rachel said, "I would get up for you to search my camel and saddle bag but it is that time of the month and it's probably better that I don't get up."

Laban said, "Oh! Please do stay seated. I don't need to deal with all of that."

After Laban's search turned up nothing. Jacob was furious. Aww man was he hot about Laban treating him and his family as if they were criminals. Jacob said to Laban, "We have done nothing to you, NOTHING AT ALL! The only thing that we have done is to treat you with respect that we never received in return from you. Now you chase us down like we are criminals and accuse us of stealing from you! Alright you searched everything and everyone, now either produce the receipts or shut up."

Jacob continued to read Laban, "I worked hard for you for too many years to be treated like this!! I have taken great care of your sheep and goats and not once has any of them died on my watch. If the wild animals did manage to kill one I replaced that dead animal with one of my animals to cover your loss and you still demanded payment from me. Never once did you take into consideration what I was going through and dealing with. I worked in the heat of the day and the cold of the night and hardly ever got any sleep between working and pleasing my wives. Fourteen of those years I worked so that I could have Rachel and Leah as my wives. It was supposed to be seven years for Rachel first but even then you tricked me and put Leah in my tent. I then worked six years so that I could have sheep and animals in order to take care of my own family and during those six years God only knows how many times you changed my coins and what you kept for yourself. You know like I know that if it had not been for God on my side I would have nothing. You would have kept everything for yourself. You know when I first arrived in the Big H and asked the shepherds at the well about you, one of them said that you were conniving and my God was he ever right. You think that I am not aware that God came to you in a dream and got on your case and told you not to act crazy but to respect me when you arrived? Hmm, it doesn't seem to me that you listened very well to what God told you!"

Laban was offended and angry because he knew that Jacob was speaking the truth. You would think that he would have been more careful especially since God had spoken to him in a dream, but let's think about this, why would Laban care what God said to him in a dream when he had all kinds of idol gods that he kept around his house? God's voice meant nothing to him because if he knew God he would not have had the false idol god statues around his house. Of course Laban got in his feelings and snapped back at Jacob and said, "Oh don't think too highly of yourself Mr. Jacob nephew son-in-law! Your wives are first my daughters and those children on those camels and donkeys are my grandchildren. All of the animals that you have are mine and everything that you own is mine. You were nothing when you came to me and you are still nothing. I made you!! Even knowing all of this, there is absolutely nothing I can do about it because you outnumber us! Let's come together, make an agreement and part ways on peaceful terms. You are taking my daughters and grandchildren so far away that I may never see them again so I want us to part ways peacefully."

Jacob thought about everything that Laban said and replied, "You know what, you are not only a con artist, but you have a lying spirit deep within you. The only thing that you have said that makes sense and that is truthful is that we should part ways peacefully because neither of us knows what tomorrow may bring."

After the two of them had gotten it all out of their systems Jacob took a big rock and made it the foundation of the big structure that he and his people would make as a monument for the agreement. Jacob placed the foundation and his relatives gathered stones to complete the monument.

Jacob and Laban still could not see eye to eye because even though Jacob and his relatives built the monument Laban wanted to name it Jegar Sahautha but since Jacob and his people had built it Jacob named it Galeed. Laban was even disrespectful of the monument and called it a heap, but he caught himself and said, "Galeed or Mizpah will be a witness to all this day that you and I, Jacob, have made an agreement to not harm each other. If either of us break this agreement than God will deal with the one that does."

Laban went on to issue a warning to Jacob and said, "If you abuse, mistreat, abandoned or neglect my daughters and my grandchildren or if you cheat on them by marrying other women, God will deal with you!"

After this they both swore by the agreement and offered a sacrifice. Afterwards, in good old-testament style, they had a nice farewell tent party. At the end of the party Laban gave that old Baptist benediction, "Now may the Lord watch between me and thee while we are absent one from another."

If you have ever wondered where that benediction came from, well now you know.

Early the next morning, about a quarter to sunrise, Laban got up and went in silently to see the grands one last time and he kissed his daughters on the forehead as he gave them a father's farewell blessing.

In accordance with the agreement that Laban and Jacob made last night, Laban and his crew rode out peacefully back to his hometown, Harran, the Big H!

49

Point(s) to Ponder: Why was Laban so upset with Jacob for leaving when Laban had already turned against him? How in the world could Laban think that all of Jacob's possessions were his? What would have happened to Jacob and his family if he had stayed with his Uncle Laban?

Take Away: When the Lord says that it is time to go and the writing is on the wall by the attitudes and behaviors of others towards you, then by all means do what you gotta do to follow the Lord's command to leave.

Prayer: Father we thank You for keeping our ears open to Your voice and our hearts available to Your guidance. We ask that as You instruct us on what to do that we would be obedient to Your will for our lives.

Ch. 4 – Genesis 32 – Jacob fears seeing Esau again.

Now that the whole mess with cousin wife's daddy is over Jacob has to face the reality that he will soon be seeing his family again and that includes Esau. Jacob wonders to himself, "I wonder if Esau still has it out for me and if my daddy is still yet holding on in the Lord or if he has gone to be with the Lord. Wow, this is going to be somethin' "tuther" because I am not the young baby face softee that I used to be. I have a family and many people serving under me. The Lord has made me a wealthy man, blessed with two wives, two side chicks and a bank of chiren. This will be more than interesting."

Jacob was so tired from all of the mess with his uncle and the stress from worrying about how he would be greeted in his hometown that he made a short stop. At this stop the angels of God were there waiting for him to let him know that everything was going to be alright. When Jacob saw them he immediately said, "This is the camp where God's angels met me, so I will name this place the Mahanaim."

Mahanaim means two hosts, so apparently from the name, God had sent two angels to meet Jacob and let him know that everything was going to be alright.

Although Jacob felt more confident after hearing the Word of the Lord from the angels he still needed to know a bit more, so he got a couple of his best men to use as scouts to go ahead of them and feel out what the temperature of his hometown was towards him, more specifically he wanted to know where Esau's head was.

Jacob sat the two men down and told them, "You are two of my best men. You are wise and have great judgement. I know that no one will be able to lie to you without you knowing. You two can smell a liar a mile away. So I need you to go to the city of Seir and go into the rural area called Edom and there you will find my family, my brother Esau."

The two men were astonished and said, "Why sir we didn't even know that you HAD a brother. You have never mentioned him in the entire time that we have been working for you."

Jacob said, "Yeah, I know. There is some history there and somethings are better kept to yourself, if ya know what I mean."

Jacob continued, "Go there and look for this man."

Jacob showed them a picture of Esau and continued, "This is my brother Esau. At least that was what he used to look like. Just look for a man with red hair all over him, even the smooth of his neck is hairy and he is also quite smelly. Once you see him approach him very gently, cause you just don't know how he is, and say this to him; your twin brother who had been staying with your mother's brother, your uncle Laban is now on his way home. He has many animals, servants, two wives and two side chicks. Those wives and side chicks have given him a bank of chiren, he wants to know if you have forgiven him and could find it in your heart to allow him to come home?"

The two men went on their way and sure enough they saw Esau as hairy as ever and when they were downwind from him, they looked at each other and said, "Wheew LAWD!!! Jacob was right. I can smell him all the way over here. Smells worse than two day old hot dog water sitting on grandma's stove!"

The two men approached Esau very gently and said, "Kind sir, we are here on behalf of your twin brother Jacob."

Esau immediately turned and looked at them in a very hasty manner. They couldn't tell from the look on his face if it was a good thing that they mentioned Jacob or not. Esau said, "You are?"

The men continued, "Yes we are. Your twin brother Jacob, had been staying with your mother's brother, your uncle Laban, and is now on his way home. He has many animals, servants, two wives and two side chicks. Those wives and side chicks have given him a bank of chiren, he wants to know if you have forgiven him and if you could find it in your heart to allow him to come home?"

The men stepped back at least two arms lengths away from Esau because they were unsure of what his reaction would be. Even though they did not know what happened between Jacob and Esau they figured it had to be something bad since Jacob would not come and speak for himself.

Esau grunted and said, "Let him know that I will come and meet him and I am bringing 400 of my own men with me."

The two men departed and went on their way back to Jacob. On the way back they said to each other, "Dude!!Now that was scary! I thought we were on a suicide mission there for a moment. That degum Esau is a fierce looking character and smells even worse. I still couldn't read him to see if he would be meeting Jacob in peace or coming to wipe us out."

When the two men reached Jacob they said, "Jacob!! You were so right. You brother is something else. That odor was horrible and we couldn't quite tell if he was angry or not. His face was like stone, smooth and solid, it never changed from the time we got there."

Jacob said, "See I told you."

The men continued, "We saw him and approached him very gently as you suggested. We held our breath as long as we could so that we could tell him what you said. We told him and he said that he would meet you and that he was bringing 400 of his own men. Now we both tried our best to figure out if he was coming in peace or in war but we still are not sure."

Jacob became visibly scared when he heard this, so much so that he forgot all about the two angels who told him it would be alright. Jacob's mind was racing so fast trying to figure out what to do. He finally decided to split his people up in two halves. He split everything from the family to the animals. Jacob was being strategic and said to himself, "If Esau comes with war on his mind and tries to do either a drive by or execution style killing, at least half of my people will have gotten away."

Jacob thought that he had better go into some serious prayer. This was a grave situation and he knew that he finally had to face his brother Esau. Jacob prayed, "Oh Lord God, MY GOD!! I need you now! When you told me to go with my mother's people, I went and while I was there you gave me all that I needed and wanted even though I had done things to show that I didn't deserve Your goodness. I had nothing when I left but You have made me so big that I have two camps of people. I ask that You would save us now from Esau. He has been waiting all of this time to take me out like Cain took out Abel! You said, oh Lord that my dependents would be like the sand of the sea which is so numerous that they can't be counted, so I am standing on Your Word!"

Jacob was so scared that he stayed another night before he broke camp and set his GPS. Jacob had taken out about 200 female camels and their babies, 40 cows and 10 bulls and 20 female donkeys and 10 male donkeys. Jacob had his servants care for each group, one servant per group and he sent them ahead of him. He told them, "Now you all go ahead of us and be sure not to bunch up. Keep a lot of space between the groups. This way if you are attacked not everyone will be attacked at the same time. Got it?"

Jacob continued, "When and if you see my brother Esau and his men coming and if he asks you if you are a part of my people and whose flocks these are, just tell him that they belong to me and that I sent them as a gift for him."

Now you know that you are scared when you start giving your goods away to your enemy in hopes of peace.

Jacob further said, "Also tell him that I am not too far behind you. He looked at all of the leaders of the flocks and told them all to say the same thing."

Jacob thought that if Esau was coming in war, by the time he passed all of the flocks that he sent ahead and knowing that it was all for him as a gift that this might calm Esau down.

Jacob then gathered his two wives, two side chicks and his eleven sons and took them to the other side of the river. After he had sent everyone away Jacob spent the night by himself. That had to be a rough night for him. He was alone and left with his fears of Esau running through his mind all night long. He was trying to figure out if he would finally pay for what he did to Esau, if his family would be saved, and if the flocks that he had sent ahead would be enough to calm Esau. He just didn't know.

When the Lord God saw how troubled Jacob was He sent an angel down to be with Jacob and they wrestled all night, right up until sunrise. The angel and Jacob wrestled all night because the angel only came for a short while to comfort Jacob but Jacob was too scared to let go. Jacob had been watching the Big H wrestling channel in his spare time so the angel had a rough battle. When the angel finally figured out that Jacob was quite a strong one and he could not get loose from him he jacked up Jacob's hip socket! Once the angel popped that socket Jacob had no choice but to let go because the pain made it impossible for Jacob to hold on. I bet that had to be some kind of pain!

The angel said, "Now let me go, it's time for me to go back. I have another assignment and you are making me late. Can't you see the sun is rising, I gotta go!"

Jacob said, "Oh no! You ain't going nowhere and leaving me down here to deal with my crazy brother all by myself! Oh no way!! I need you to bless me with strength and power to do what I need to do and that depends on how Esau comes at me. After you bless me I'll let you go."

The angel said, "Well, in that case, tell me your name."

Jacob said, "Jacob."

The angel said, "You know what? The way that you wrestled with me all night, and the way that you have dealt with people, namely your Uncle Laban, and especially since you love God so much, your name is no longer Jacob."

Jacob said, "Well, what is your name?"

I do believe that at this point and after wrestling with this angel all night, I would have asked the angel what's MY new name way before asking what is his name! I think Jacob missed an opportunity.

The angel asked Jacob, "Why do you need to know my name? That's not what I came here for. My name is of no importance to you. Now let me bless you so that I can get to my next assignment."

So the angel blessed Jacob and went on to his next assignment. After the angel left Jacob felt the need to name the spot where all of this had taken place. Jacob said, "I believe that I will call this place Peniel because after wrestling all last night I know that, that couldn't have been anybody BUT GOD! I have been with God, face to face and I didn't die. WOW! That's a big deal. I have heard of people trying to see His face and they didn't make it. He let ME live! Ya know I feel some kinda special!"

After this the sun came on up in the background, the birds chirped and the angels sang. All of that peace and harmony stuff, but Jacob carried the pain of the night with him in the form of a limp because the angel jacked that hip up! Jacob could not blame the angel for his hip being out of socket, because in all actuality it was Jacob's fault. He should have just let go of the angel and manned up to meet his brother Esau.

The strangest thing that came out of this is that to this very day it is said that people from Israel will not eat the tendon that leads to the hip socket because of how the angel jacked up Jacob's hip!

Point (s) to Ponder: Why was Jacob so quick to forget what the angels had just told him when he was just a few miles down the road? Didn't they tell him that everything was going to be alright? Why did he allow his fears to rule over him, when in fact he had many men and the Lord had increased him and was with him? How did the angel bless Jacob?

Take Away: When the Lord gives you a word, whether it comes directly from His angels, through a prophet, friend or in prayer do not take it lightly, but rather hold on to it because you may not need it at that particular moment, however you will eventually need to fall back on that Word at some point in your life for strength and maybe even for dear life.

Prayer: Father in the name of Your son Yeshua (Jesus) we ask that You send us an encouraging and strengthening Word because the times that we are in present themselves as our Esau and we need Your help to not only meet the challenges but to overcome the fear and anxiety that comes with them. We ask this so that we may come out of this standing in the place of victory as You would have us to.

Ch. 5 – Genesis 33 – The twins meet again

Just as Jacob was really beginning to feel that Holy Ghost confidence lo and behold he saw Esau coming his way and as he told the two servants he would, Esau was riding 400 deep. (He had his 400 men with him.)

In the previous chapter we thought that Jacob had sent the wives and children away, but he only had them to sleep separate from him in case Esau came in the night to attack. So when Jacob saw Esau in the distance, he put his plan into action. He split the bank of children between Rachel, Leah and the two side chick servants. The order that Jacob had them riding lets me know the order of importance. Jacob made the two side chick servants and their children ride out first, next was Leah and her chiren and then Rachel and Jacob. He made sure that he protected Rachel above all else. When Esau was closer to Jacob and his people Jacob ran ahead of everyone and bowed down at least seven times before Esau even reached him.

In Biblical numerology seven stands for completion. It seems that Jacob was bowing before his brother to say let the past stay in the past, the past is complete and let's move forward. This just might have worked because when Esau got closer to Jacob he jumped off his ride and ran to meet Jacob. When Jacob saw this he thought for sure Esau was coming to take revenge.

Jacob was still on his seventh bow and he said, "Father in heaven, You said that everything was going to be alright, you even sent another angel here to comfort me last night and to bless me, I ask now that You would release that blessing and calm my brother Esau so that when he reaches me he will be peaceful and not full of old rage and hate. Lord if he does come with revenge in his heart PLEASE let him only take it out on me and not my family."

When Esau finally reached Jacob he grabbed him and gave him the biggest hug. He literally picked Jacob up off the ground, held him and kissed him on the neck. This was so touching that both Jacob and Esau cried tears of joy.

Esau said, "My brother, my twin, JACOB!! Man you are a sight for MY eyes. After the way you left over 14 years ago I didn't think that I would EVER see you again. WOW!! It's really you! When your two servants came to see me and told me that you were on your way home and asked if I would forgive you I could hardly contain myself. I had forgiven you shortly after you left. I kinda missed you calling me funk horrible! Ya know the kitchen just isn't the same without you, but from how shredded you are and all of your people and family I can tell that the kitchen is the last place that you have been!!"

Jacob was so happy to hear his brother talk this way and the way that his brother embraced and kissed him wiped all of the fear away. Jacob had been worrying himself sleepless for no reason. Jacob replied to Esau, "Bru-tha!! I am so happy to see you also and more especially happy to see that you are not still mad with me for how mother and I did you. Thank you for forgiving me."

Esau replied, "No worries, no problem. Hey man I see all of these shortys over there who are they? Are they all yours?"

Jacob answered, "Yes, they are all my wives, side chicks and my bank of chiren. God has been truly good to me and blessed me even in the worst of situations."

When Jacob told Esau who they were they all came over to meet Esau. They came over in the order that Jacob had set in order to protect Rachel if something bad went down with Esau. First the side chicks and their children came to introduce themselves to Esau and next came Leah and her children. After Leah and her children Rachel came over to Jacob's side and they both bowed before Esau. Esau said to Jacob, "Who in the world would have ever thought that my little brother, the kitchen master, would have all of this. And you have such beautiful women. I guess beauty truly does run in the family."

Esau looked around some more and said, "Bruh, what's up with all of the animals that I saw on my way to see you?"

Jacob said, "Well you see I wasn't exactly sure what was going on in your head regarding me, so I thought that I would give you all of these animals as a way to calm you down if you were still mad with me."

Esau stepped back a bit and looked around and said, "Ya know that is very thoughtful of you and all but please keep them for yourself, believe me when I tell you that I have more than enough."

Jacob was determined to give them to Esau. He insisted that Esau take them. Jacob was still scared because he remembered how much of a strategist Esau was, so Jacob continued and said, "Aww come on now! I have come all of this way to see you and to bring you gifts. If you truly have forgiven me in your heart please take the animals as my gift to you. Dude, you don't understand! Seeing you right now is almost like seeing God face to face. God has been so good to me and has answered my prayers, so please accept this gift."

After Esau heard this his heart was truly touched so he gave in and accepted the animals as a gift. Esau said, "Come on bruh let's make our way back to the house. I am sure that everyone will be so happy to see you and to meet your family. You know you've been like a ghost, so let's get it. I will go first, me and my men, and we will announce you to the town as we enter! Ya know, sort of a welcome escort."

Jacob wanted to go home as quickly as he could but he thought about his children and the baby animals. He thought that if the trip was too fast it would be too much for them, especially the baby animals so he told Esau, "You go on ahead and we will move at our usual slow pace in order for my children and animals to be properly taken care of. We will eventually get there. Hey, we may be slow, but we will show."

Esau said, "Hey I get it! I understand what you are saying, but look I gotta get back, I got some things in the works and need to be there for some important meetings, plus my many wives will miss me if I am not home soon, if ya know what I mean. BUT, just because you are my little brother and I love you I will leave some of my men here to help you out."

Jacob thought that this was unusual and suspect. He still wasn't feeling Esau. Jacob may have been skeptical because he had just finished dealing with sneaky conniving Laban and he remembered how his ear hustling mother's scheme got all of this started in the first place. Jacob had some serious trust issues, but rightfully so. So Jacob replied to Esau, "Naw man that's alright. I got this. Just seeing your face and feeling your love is enough. You and your men go on ahead and I will see you in Seir. I bet that city has changed a lot since I have been gone."

Esau said, "Yes, that part!"

And with those words, Esau and his 400 men were off, leaving a huge cloud of dust that eventually settled on Jacob and his camp. After Esau pulled off, Jacob set the GPS for Succoth. When he finally got there he set up some temporary housing for his camp and had his men to build sheds for the animals. The sheds were something new in this area and because of this the place was named Succoth which literally means sheds.

Once Jacob was settled he and Rachel sat down and had a long talk. Jacob said, "Honey, did you see how the Lord worked that out with Esau? I mean I couldn't have asked for anything more!! I worried and wrestled with an angel all night because I was so scared, BUT GOD did what He always does, steps in right on time!!"

Rachel replied, "Yes, yes, yes! God did that!! I knew that you were really worried and scared for our safety because you sent us to stay on the other side of the river and you slept all alone. Thank God that Esau's heart towards you has changed, but I did notice you giving Esau the side eye a couple of times. Honey, just trust the Lord. He has had your back all of this time, why would He stop now? Why would He leave you hanging?"

This is the story of how Jacob and all of his people arrived in his hometown without having one hair on their heads bothered. Jacob was now in Shechem which was in the land of Canaan. He set up his camp right outside of the city on land that the Sons of Hamor, the father of Shechem used to own. Jacob paid them 100 silver coins to have this land for him and his people. Once Jacob purchased the property and everyone was settled in, he did like his father Isaac and Isaac's father Abraham and built an altar. In all that Jacob had endured to get to this point he saw God as the mighty God of Israel so he named the altar El-Elohe-Israel which means Mighty is the God of Israel.

Point (s) to Ponder: In this chapter we witnessed God breaking down a barrier of hatred that Esau had for his brother Jacob. Jacob worried so much over this situation, but the main thing that he did was to pray and ask God to touch his brother's heart. Do you think that Jacob is on point when he still feels uneasy about Esau and his motives or is this a developed trust issue that belongs solely to Jacob?

Take Away: When we are able to confront and eliminate issues of the past that have caused harm to others and ourselves we should take the opportunity and make full use of it. We never know if that opportunity will come again and we do not know if once we leave the presence of the person or people that we need to resolve these issues with, will these individuals still be around later. If God gives opportunity to rectify past events, take full advantage of it knowing that clearing the sludge of the past is not only for you, but for all involved.

Prayer: Father we thank You today that You have shown us how to settle past issues. We ask that all involved would receive us and that we in turn will receive them. Thank You for allowing us to clear our hearts and minds so that we are able to focus on building newness in relationships and in our hearts.

Ch. 6 – Genesis 34 – Baby girl is stalked, raped and kidnapped

Just like Lot, Jacob didn't give any consideration to the type of people that lived in the land where he chose to settle. He did not do his due diligence, scout it out or even check it out and my God yes, as he suspected things had greatly changed over the past 14-20 years.

Jacob had a bank of chiren and of those he had one girl and her name was Dinah. Dinah was a very pretty young lady. Her dominant genes had to come from her father Jacob because her mother was lazy eyed Leah, and we all know that lazy eyed means ugly! Dinah was pretty like her aunt Rachel and often times it was thought that Rachel was her mother.

The police report and newspaper articles state that on or about eleven o'clock on a Thursday, Dinah left home to go and hang out with a few people that she had met in the town. They had planned to arrive at the corner of Shechem Town Center Blvd and Gate Parkway around eleven hundred hours to have lunch and go shopping at the Shechem Town Center and at the Canaan Mall.

Per the Uber driver, he dropped Dinah off at exactly eleven hundred hours at that same corner location. He remembers seeing her standing on that corner as he drove away. The story continues with Dinah's account. As she was standing there she noticed one of the big dawgs staring at her. She recognized this man to be Shechem who was not only the son of the man (Hamor) that Dinah's father Jacob had purchased their land from but as well his father owned and named the Town Center after him. Shechem stated that he

67

had seen Dinah before and that he fell hard for her. Shechem was not an honorable young man. He was a Hivite and because of his status as a dignitary he pretty much got what he wanted and when he wanted it. He had hollered at Dinah before but she ignored him due to his reputation and besides that Leah and Jacob told her not to mess with the locals.

Shechem was much like the serpent in Genesis 3, always swaggin' around town trying to get something started. Shechem said, "Hey gurl! Hey there! Look at me! I know that you hear me. HEY!! I have hollered at you before and you just keep it movin'! Do you know who I am? When **I** speak **YOU** answer! What **IZ** your problem?"

Dinah was already aware of who he was and more importantly what he was capable of, so she did not reply or even look his way, she just kept it movin'. Dinah wondered to herself, "Where are the others that I was supposed to meet here? We were supposed to meet here over 10 minutes ago. Lord please let them hurry up this Shechem situation is very uncomfortable and seems to be escalating."

Dinah stood there waiting for the other young ladies to arrive. Even though Jacob and Leah had told Dinah not to mess with the locals, Dinah thought that they only meant the men. She had made friends with a couple of the young ladies from the area. Little did Dinah know that these young ladies were related to Shechem and they set her up to arrive on that corner for their cousin Shechem! So in the meantime Shechem saw how alone she was and thought that this was his perfect opportunity to have his way with her. He thought to himself, "I gotta give my cousins their props. They set this up perfectly. I couldn't have done better myself!"

In that instance Shechem grabbed Dinah from the back, covered her mouth and drug her into an alley, and proceeded to forcibly rape her! This is outrageous, despicable and certainly beyond unacceptable!! Shechem had his way with Dinah and carried on like a mad man! I hope for his sake that he thinks it is worth it because he just does not know whose daughter he has messed with, but guess what, he will certainly find out and sooner than he thinks!!

Most rapist flee the scene and threaten their victims, but not this nut case NAW, Shechem is crazy because what happens next is unbelievable. After Shechem violently raped Dinah, he then fell head over heels in love with her and started acting as if they are a couple and had been a couple for a long time. What a warped mind! Shechem told Dinah, "I would like to take you out for dinner and buy you the biggest diamond so that we can be married."

Crazy man Shechem took it even further and forced Dinah to come with him to his house. He kidnapped Dinah and held her against her will. Once He is at his house Shechem goes to his father Hamor and says, "Dad, I met this young lady named Dinah. She is the only daughter of that new family that you sold land to. As a matter of fact she is downstairs right now. I would like for you to convince her father to let me marry her."

Hamor looked at Shechem and said, "What have you done now? Every time that I turn around I am getting you out of some mess that you have created. Why should I have to go to this girl's father? That alone lets me know that you are lying and the truth ain't in you. You are lying again! Boy, I am so sick of you and your drama! What is really going on here? What have you done?"

In the meantime, word from the street got back to Jacob what had happened to his baby girl Dinah. All of Jacob's sons were out working at the time Jacob found out, so he figured he would let them come home from work and then tell them. In between the time that the boys came in from work and when Jacob would tell them, Hamor had the nerve to pull up on Jacob's doorstep. Hamor knocked on the door and when the servant opened the door the servant was shocked to see him. We all know that if the news had spread throughout the town then Jacob's entire household knew what had happened. As the servant brought Hamor to Jacob he stared at him and gave him the once over and then said, "Right this way."

Now when the servant left their presence, he went back to the kitchen and told the others what was happening. They of course, sent him back to ear hustle the conversation.

Jacob held it together as best he could and said, "Yes what can I do for you?"

Hamor said, "I am here regarding that little tiny incident that happened with my son and your daughter."

Jacob was furious and said, "LITTLE TINY INCIDENT! How dare you! Your no good undisciplined sick warped minded son RAPED my only daughter and you pull up on me, in my home, and to my face talkin' about the little tiny incident! Man I ought to…"

Hamor quickly cut Jacob off and said, "I am sorry I really don't meant to make light of it, but from the way your daughter was dressed, just standing on the corner like that and along with how fine she is, well what do you expect?!

Jacob lunged at him!

Hamor back away quickly and continued, "AND the fact that she was alone tells me that either she may have been asking for it or had seen my son before and wanted his attention. He is quite handsome, takes after me! BUT nevertheless, I am here to ask that you allow my son to marry your only daughter? He is head over heels in love with her and he said that he fell in love with her after he raped her. Strange boy!"

Jacob said, "Strange isn't even the word for that big piece of cow poop! And where is my daughter? Why hasn't she returned home?"

As Hamor and Jacob were talking Jacob's sons were off of work and on their way home when they heard all the commotion in town, especially as they slowly rode by with the windows down. They heard people saying, "Man when Jacob's sons find out what Shechem did to Dinah they will have his head. Them boys don't play the radio about their sister!"

Another said, "Yes that part right there! AND Shechem is holding her at his father's house and now says he wants to marry her. Shechem has raped too many young girls around here, I certainly hope that he gets dealt with this time."

Another said, "Um huh. I do believe that this will be the last time that, that little sawed off spoiled entitled little runt bothers anyone ever again!"

When Jacob's boys heard this they hit sport mode on the transpo whip and went flying home.

Hamor was still talking and said, "Not only am I asking that you give Dinah to Shechem, but that you allow our people to intermarry, ya know you can have our women and we can have yours."

This further outraged Jacob. Hamor just didn't understand how Jacob and his people looked upon rape. It was demeaning, disgusting and an act against God.

Just about this time you could hear the screech from the transpo whip as it pulled up outside. Jacob's boys burst into the house ready to go take revenge and when they saw Hamor they went straight for him because they knew if Hamor had stopped Shechem years ago from raping girls this would not have happened to their sister Dinah. Simeon, Leah's son, spoke up and said, "What is this dog doing here? Hamor you have some nerve showing your face and you have the nerve to ask for your dog of a son to marry my precious sister after what he has done, I will kill you and that dog myself."

Jacob stepped in and said, "Hold up, hold up! I got this. I GOT this."

Hamor said, "I don't mean no harm by coming here! Please, please, you don't know how hard I have tried with that son of mine. Always having to spend my hard earned money bailing him out of drama anywhere from gambling to rape."

This time Levi, one of Leah's others sons, spoke up and said, "Maybe, just maybe if you had spent your hard earned money on getting your son some mental health counseling and inpatient treatment instead of encouraging him by buying him out of trouble we wouldn't be here now."

Hamor felt that he should really humble himself since he was surrounded by these big corn bread eating sons of Jacob. Hamor continued and said, "You are so right. Looking back over the situations I should have gotten him help instead of throwing a band aid made out of money over it. It's just that he is my only son and heir! I want you all to know that I will pay anything, any amount of money if you would let my son marry Dinah. Money is no object and I have other sources of wealth available also. I will even change the name on the town center to Dinah and Shechem Town Center! How's that sound?"

Jacob spoke and said, "Hamor, if you would step outside for a moment and let me and my sons discuss your offer?"

Hamor replied, "Of course sir, of course! Take your time."

Jacob and his sons put their heads together and discussed the entire situation. Word on the street has it that Leah's sons wanted to outright kill Shechem for what he had done and kill his father Hamor for allowing him to do this to so many girls over the years. The side chick's sons were game for whatever. They would kill them both, if that was the majority decision or they would allow them to marry, however the wind blew was cool with them. Now, it was Jacob and Rachel's son that came up with the master plan. This plan was filled with wisdom and strategy!

Jacob called Hamor back in to the study where the discussion was taking place and said, "Okay, we have come to a decision on this matter."

Hamor was panting like a dog and said, "Yes, yes?"

Jacob continued, "Marriage would be great…"

Hamor interrupted, "Yes, yes! I thought that you would see it my way and I am so happy that you did! Why let your daughter walk around a disgraced and contaminated woman who no longer has her virginity, when she can be made whole through marriage? Why no other man would want her anyways after all of this. I am so glad that we could reach an agreement. My son will be overjoyed by the news."

Jacob held back his anger because he knew of the bigger picture and said, "As I was saying before you so rudely interrupted me, marriage would be great, because your son Shechem has shamed Dinah and the great possibility is that no other man would now want her not only because her virginity has been stolen but because she has been raped and the emotional luggage that comes with being raped. She will probably never trust another man let alone let a man touch her! HOWEVER, we cannot allow our precious Dinah to marry your son or for that matter any of our women to marry your men unless you all become circumcised as we are. If you and the men in your society agree to this then Dinah can marry Shechem and your men can marry our women. How does that sound? Remember if that is not good enough we will take our Dinah, pack all of our resources and leave the area."

Hamor did not want the local economy to suffer because of his foolish son, so he agreed and said, "That sounds like a plan. I will get right on it. I will not only make sure that Shechem and I are circumcised but I will call a town meeting today and get all the men in town on board with this. Thank you for being so understanding about this tiny little incident!"

Hamor left immediately and told Shechem the good news. Shechem was overjoyed and ran in to tell Dinah, whom he was holding captive. He said, "Dinah darling, my father has spoken with your father and brothers and they have agreed to let me marry you! Isn't that awesome news!"

Dinah looked at him and thought to herself, "Bruh, you just don't know my brothers like I do. They are very protective of me, their only sister, so there is something in the works. OH YEAH, it's going down!"

Dinah, with twisted lips and a side eye look on her face, finally spoke to Shechem and said, "Sure that sounds like a great plan, for YOU, you piece of poop imbecile!"

Shechem thought for sure that he had everyone's buy in, so he headed straight over to the outpatient clinic and set up his circumcision appointment for the same day. In the meantime, Hamor held the town meeting and said, "Brother, brothers I have called this meeting today to discuss the men among us. These men are just like us, flesh and bone and their blood runs red and warm just like ours. I would like to ask that we make them full pledged citizens with all rights and honors as ourselves. Then we can intermarry with their beautiful women. We can't lose by doing this because they have big money and all kinds of assets that would really give our local economy a boost. Although there is one catch…"

One of the councilmen stated, "I knew that there was more to it. You call us in here trying to be all sneaky and present all of this positivity but we all know what your son did. This is a pattern, he rapes a girl you call a meeting. When will you get him the help he needs? That is what we should be voting on today! All in favor of getting Shechem inpatient mental health assistance say yay!"

The vote of YAY was so loud it could be heard outside of the Town Hall.

Hamor stepped up and took the microphone back and said, "Look that is all good and I appreciate the concern for my son, however I will make sure that he gets mental health assistance, as a matter of fact he is at the outpatient center as I speak, I will call over and add that on to his surgery order."

The men said all in one voice, "SURGERY?"

Hamor said, "Yes, surgery. That is the catch, that we all get surgically circumcised. That's not so hard is it? We have all talked about this before but just never made a decision and now this great opportunity is before us, so let's all just go over and get it done. Then we can have those beautiful women. Those women are not going to touch us without this being done, so what do you say? Let's vote?"

The men looked at each other. Some were shaking their heads no and others yes so they took a vote and it passed by an extremely narrow margin.

All the men went over to outpatient and had themselves circumcised. The Outpatient clinic was so overwhelmed that the staff thought it was another pandemic. The women of the town felt some kind of way about this and were overheard saying, "Look at this! Well, I guess that we are a monkey's uncle! Look at what these men are lined up to do just to have a chance to be with one of the new women in town. OMG! As if we are not good enough!"

Another local town's women said, "Yeah, isn't this a blimp! You do know that they are spitting in our face and I agree, it's as if they are telling us that we are not good enough. They wouldn't get circumcised for us, no matter how many times we had to run to the OB GYN because of it. I'm done! I'm just done!"

The men were given aftercare instructions and sent home. They were told no heavy lifting, no swimming, and no beach activity for at least two weeks and definitely they could have no sexual activity of any kind for at least six weeks. So basically all that they could do was lay around, watch movies and chill until they healed.

As the story is told it was on that third day. Yes, it seems that great things happen on the Third day! But on THIS particular third day, after the circumcision procedures Hamor and all of the town's men were heard moaning and groaning from the pain. This was the perfect time for the other part of the plan that the Jacob's sons had come up with in Jacob's absence. Simeon and Levi were ready to go into action. This was a scheme that belonged solely to Leah's sons. I guess Dinah really did know her brothers better than anyone else, even Jacob.

While the men of the town were at their lowest point following the circumcision, Simeon and Levi took it upon themselves to go in and revenge their sister's rape! They went into that town in straight gangsta mode! The story on the street is that them boys had all types of weapons and walked up in there like they were agents of the Cartel or something. They killed every man in that town, that day! Literally, they left no man standing or alive!

After they took care of the town's men, Simeon and Levi went straight to Hamor and Shechem's house. Aww man, the crime scene at their house was so bloody that forensics couldn't make heads or tale of it. After Simeon and Levi killed those two, they searched the house and found the underground bunker where Shechem had hidden Dinah. When they open that thing up and saw what shape their sister was in, they started crying and apologizing for what had happened to her. They grabbed her up and carried her out of that mad house and had one of the servants to take her to the hospital. Simeon and Levi did not take Dinah to the hospital themselves because they still had a lot of work to do to complete the revenge plan.

If that wasn't bad enough, once Simeon and Levi finished their killing spree the rest of Jacob's boys came in and looted the city like they were far right wing extremist during a peaceful BLM protest in 2020. They looted, broke windows, started fires and took whatever pleased their eyes. There wasn't a jewelry store, bank or electronic store that hadn't been robbed. They took all the animals, women and children. After this they went into the private homes, made the women open the private safes and took whatever they wanted. All of the men in the town were dead so there was no one to stop them. This spree went on for at least five days.

The only reason that all of the thievery stopped was because Jacob finally went out looking for them. He had not seen them since all the men were circumcised. He rode through the town and was blown away at what he saw, but what really blew his mind was

78

that he caught Levi and Simeon red handed. Jacob looked at them both and said, "What in the world have you done?!! Now everyone around will hate MY name because of your violence. Did you ever stop to think that these men had family and friends? What if the other Canaanites and Perizzites caught wind of this and decided that they would come over and dead you and all of us because of what you have done? We do not have enough people to wage a war with them! What were you thinking?"

Simeon and Levi both looked at their father, Jacob and said, "What have we done?! What did Shechem do to our sister? What did Hamor do for his son? They did not know who they were messing with and that there is one thing in this life that they will not do and that we will not tolerate and that is to rape our sister or treat her like a whore!! I do not know why any of them thought that they could do it and get away with it. NOT ON OUR WATCH! Ain't that right brothers?"

All of Jacob's sons answered in harmony, "And you know that!"

This story was told in grade school classes throughout Jacob's camp to help both boys and girls, men and women to understand the far reaching effects of rape. While Dinah was in the hospital recovering she received mental health counseling to help her wade through the baggage of rape. Everyone agreed that that they were thankful to God that she did not become pregnant from the rape.

After Dinah was released from the hospital, she received requests to speak on many well-known television and radio talk shows. Dinah finally formed a team and went on a speaking tour and started a movement for women who had been sexually abused, molested and raped. #DINAH

Point (s) to Ponder: Why didn't Jacob provide more care and security for his only daughter Dinah? Because of the previous trust issues that Jacob had shouldn't that have made him more aware of his surroundings, especially since he was the head man in charge? Were Jacob's sons wrong for the way they avenged their sister's rape?

Take Away: This chapter tells a biblical story but also highlights what women have been dealing with for centuries at the hands of men. What more can be done to destroy the view that some men have of women and children? Was Shechem's behaviors passed down to him and why didn't his father get him mental health assistance and let him face his consequences rather than buying him out of trouble? Why was Hamor so quick to blame Dinah for his son's actions?

Prayer: Father we thank You today for providing protection for the many women and children in the world. We ask that You would keep harmful and violent men away and that for those that have harmed someone in any manner that they would receive immediate consequences for their actions.

Ch #7 – Genesis 35 – Movin' to Bethel – three die

After all of the drama and dust had settled from what happened to Dinah and the destructive aftermath that followed, Jacob needed to hear from the Lord. Jacob was extremely concerned about if the neighboring town's people would try to attack them due to how his sons avenged the dishonoring of their only sister Dinah. Jacob spoke to Rachel and said, "Bae, you know that I am very unsure of where we stand with the Canaanites and the Perizzites, and I feel eerily uncomfortable about everything here. The boys really did a job on this town by killing all of the men, kidnapping the women and children and looting every bank, home safe, electronic store and jewelry store in this town. I am just not sure if the Canaanites and Perizzites will try to revenge all that went down. They may see us as a threat to their way of life and, after what the boys did, they may see us as a threat to their very existence! I'm just not sure what to do, which way to turn or go. We need to pray, because I need to hear a word from the Lord on this right away. We are most likely in severe danger!"

Just as Jacob and Rachel finished praying the Lord had called down to Jacob with a message and answer to his prayer, the Lord said, "Jacob I have heard you and Rebekah's prayer and I feel where you are coming from. You are wise to be concerned because the neighboring people, the Canaanites and the Perizzites, are scheming and planning to attack and kill every last one of you! Evil is lurking beyond your camp. I need you to get your stuff together and ride out to Bethel. Once you are there stay for a little while and build an altar. After you build the altar I want you to remember how God came to you the very first night after you left your mother and father's house to escape

Esau. You were on your own and fearing for your life just as you are now. Before you leave you need to clean up the people among you and have them to give your head of security any false gods and items that they carry for luck. These things were mostly brought in by the kidnapped women and children but there are a few of your people that have been with you a while that also have them. After all of this is done, pack up and ride out!"

When Jacob heard this he called a meeting with his family and the head of security and told them what God had spoken to him. He gave the following orders to be carried out, "I just finished speaking with God and he told me that we need to leave this place immediately because evil is lurking beyond our camp! He said for us to go to Bethel, but before we do there are two things that MUST happen, number one is that all of the false and idol gods that the people have among them must be turned in along with anything that they hold on to bring them luck. When you are collecting these remember that it is just not the foreigners among us, but some of our people have them too. And the second thing is that all of the people must take a nice hot shower or bath and put on their Sunday's best because we are going to Bethel and we can't roll up representin' God looking like a bunch of skanks. We gotta roll out in style, smelling and looking good! Now once we get there, I will build an altar to my God because every time things have looked and gone crazy in my life He was there for me and had my back even when I didn't deserve it! "

Just as the Lord had instructed, all of the people turned over their false and idol gods. There were women and young girls that turned in earrings that they wore for luck.

Some of the men had rabbit's feet or pocket knives for good luck and they turned them in. Once all of these items were brought to Jacob he took the back hoe and dug a deep hole near the oak tree at Shechem Town Center and buried them there, under one of the oak trees. With this being done Jacob spoke to all of the people in his camp and told them, "Now that we have gotten rid of those things that do not please the almighty God we are all in sync and must put our trust in God and God alone, for it is He that has protected me all of my life and it is He that will protect us now against what lies beyond our camp. Even though my sons were righting a wrong that was done to their sister there are many beyond this camp that do not agree with how it was done and in turn want to take revenge on us. So before we leave let us all pray for God's protection, for His angels to watch over us and for the hearts of the people outside of this camp to be changed towards us once we head out of here for Bethel."

The entire camp said in unison, "Amen, Amen, and Amen! So let it be unto us."

It was so loud that the neighboring Canaanites and Perizzites heard it. It was reported as an unidentified boom on the nightly news.

Once Jacob and his camp pulled out in route to Bethel the air became very thick and silent. Jacob did not know what to expect, but he knew that he had done what the Lord instructed and that he and his camp had prayed and were on one accord. The head of security ran over to Jacob and said, "I have sent scouts ahead to check things out before we get so far out here and so far the report is good."

Jacob said, "That was a smart move and greatly appreciated, but I feel confident that God has us."

As Jacob's camped drove past the inner city, suburbs and rural area of the towns where the Canaanites and Perizzites lived it seems that the people who lived there were fearful of them. Once the people saw them they ran inside. Jacob had on his car radio and the news reporter and even the DJ's stated, "Jacob and his sons are coming through the area like a strong westerly wind. We are unsure of if they are coming to our area to bring destruction or if they are passing through, so we are advising you to hunker down in your homes. Protect your windows and doors and bring any outdoor items that you want to keep, into your garage. Make sure that pets are in and plants are covered. This is not to be taken lightly, government officials have issued a Defcon 1 alert meaning we are in a maximum readiness state, and there is danger at your door. So stay inside and stay ready for whatever."

Wow!! It seems that God had answered Jacob's prayer and the surrounding town's people were running and hiding like little punks. The head of security pulled up to Jacob and gave him the brotha man head nod and said, "That's what I'm talking about!! Won't He do it!"

Jacob nodded back and said, "Yes He will!! You got that right."

When Jacob and his people finally arrived at Bethel, Jacob was obedient and built an altar to the Lord as he said he would. He built the altar in the exact same spot that he stopped on the very first night that he left running from Esau. This time Jacob named the altar El-Bethel which meant God of Bethel. Jacob and his people worshipped and thanked the Lord for how he paralyzed the Canaanites and Perizzites as they passed through!

Just as they were getting into deep praise and worship and the praise team was taking them into the presence of the Lord, Rachel's nurse, Deborah, passed out. At first no one paid her any attention, because she was known to go into the presence of the Lord so deep that she would pass out under His power, but this time that was not the case!! It seems that all of the excitement was too much for poor Deborah and she actually had a massive heart attack and stayed in the presence of the Lord this time. Loosing Deborah was a huge loss for Jacob's camp. Deborah was a very powerful prayer warrior and she was a nurse. She would be missed greatly. Loosing Deborah was also a big personal loss for Rachel because she was pregnant and was now without a nurse to help her with delivering the baby.

The arrangements were made for the deceased prayer warrior and nurse Deborah, and she was buried under an oak tree that was just outside of the town of Bethel.

Has anyone else noticed that Jacob liked using oak trees to bury things for some odd reason?

Rachel named the oak tree Allon-Bacuth which means weeping oak. Kind of befitting I'd say!

After the home going service and repass in Paddan Aram were all over and Jacob had returned to his camp, the Lord had a word for Jacob. The Lord spoke to Jacob and said, "When you were born you were named Jacob, which means heel, you have proven yourself to be more than a Jacob so I am changing your name to Israel which means "Wrestler of God." You wrestled with my angel and with men and have come out on top each time, so you are My wrestler."

God had more to say, "I am the only true and Strong God and I say that you will have more children and you will continue to grow and flourish in all things. Your children will become nations and kings. The land that you are standing on that I gave to Abraham and Isaac is now your land. I am giving it to you and you will pass it down to your children."

After God finished speaking, His presence left that place where He spoke to Jacob and of course Jacob felt the need to build a stone pillar, much like he did the first night when he was running from Esau. Jacob went a little further this time, he took some wine as a drink offering and poured it on the pillar and he also anointed the pillar with anointing oil. Jacob did this as a way of dedicating the pillar to God because this is where God personally spoke to him on two occasions in Bethel, which is God's house.

Jacob gathered his people up and they moved out again heading towards the town of Ephrath. It seems that this trip had a lot going on because just as they were a little ways out from Ephrath Rachel started having sharp labor pains. I mean the pains were so sharp and hard that the whole camp had to pull over and stop. They had just buried Rachel's nurse Deborah, so one of her sister Leah's nurses stepped up to help her out.

Rachel was crying and asking for her beloved Jacob to come and be with her, for this was a very hard labor and delivery. Jacob came running into the delivery room and looked at Rachel crying in pain and it broke his little heart. He ran over and grabbed her hand and kissed her on the forehead just as he had done when he first met her at the well. He thought to himself, "Rachel had one other child birth for me, but this seems oddly different. Something just doesn't seem right!"

Jacob asked Rachel, "How you doing? Are they taking good care of you care of?"

Rachel replied, "Yes, they are taking great care of me, but I feel very odd. This is very different than the other birth. The nurse says that my blood pressure is extremely high and they are unable to bring it down, this has been going on for a little while now. It actually started when I was around 5 months in to the pregnancy. I didn't tell you because I did not want you to worry. You have enough on your plate."

Jacob said, "Honey baby, I never have too much on my plate that I can't see about you. You are my one and only sweet baby. Anything concerning you concerns me."

Rachel continued, "Jacob, my eyes are very blurry and my head is poppin', put that together with the labor pains and I feel like a dirty dish rag!"

Jacob called for the nurse. The nurse came back in and asked to speak with Jacob outside of the delivery room. The nurse said, "Sir, if we are not able to get her blood pressure down, she runs the risk of stroke, heart attack or maybe even death. We are doing all that we can so I suggest that you pray because it is out of our hands."

Jacob looked back into the room at Rachel, started crying and ran to the chapel to pray! Jacob prayed mightily because he did not want to lose his sweet love Rachel. Jacob prayed, "My Father and my God, I know that You can see what is going on down here with my love Rachel and our child. I ask that You send Your healing power into the delivery room and lower Rachel's blood pressure to normal. I ask that You would cause her entire body to function as you created it to function. I do not want to lose Rachel or the baby so I ask that You would step in and have Your way!"

After Jacob prayed he layed on the altar before the Lord on behalf of his wife and child. Jacob felt a release in his spirit to go back into the delivery room. So Jacob wiped the tears from his eyes and collected himself. He wanted to be strong for Rachel. Just as he walked into the delivery room he heard the nurse tell Rachel, "You have nothing to fear the baby is just about here."

And a few moments later the nurse said, "You are the proud parents of a boy!"

Jacob and Rachel were overjoyed and kissed. Jacob squeezed her hand and said, "You did great baby! Thank you and I love you!"

Just as Jacob said that the monitors started beeping because Rachel was hemorrhaging. Even though Rachel's body was shutting down she was determined to name the baby. Rachel held the baby, kissed it and said with her last dying breath, "Your name is Ben-oni, because you my son have caused me great pain!"

Jacob looked at them both and said, "As his father and your husband I am changing his name to Benjamin because he is a son of good fortune!"

A few moments later the machines flat lined and Rachel was gone on home to be with the Lord. Jacob's sobbing and crying could be heard throughout the hospital and camp. His heart had broken into a thousand pieces at the loss of his beloved Rachel. His mind flashed back to their first moments and their last moments. Jacob took a couple of days to himself and he left baby boy Benjamin in the nurse's care.

After three days had passed Jacob had a wake and a home going service for Rachel. Jacob spared no expense in making sure that nothing but the best was used to send Rachel off. The service was said to be longer than the televised services of the two divas of soul music! Rachel's service was live streamed, televised, on the radio AND all media platforms were taken over to broadcast her service live. Rachel had a solid gold casket and was clothed in a gold spun dress and red bottom 6" heels. It was a sight to see and is still talked about to this day.

Jacob built an especially large headstone with the caption, 'Here lies my beautiful beloved wife who is the first love of my life. She gave me two sons, plenty of love, consideration and kindness. We were one, a team and she always had my back! I will always love and keep her in my heart."

Jacob also set up a huge pillar as a grave marker.

Do you remember when the angel changed Jacob's name to Israel, but he continued to be called Jacob? Well, after the death of Rachel everyone started calling Jacob, Israel.

Israel, even though he was still grieving, decided it was time to continue on his journey to his hometown. He had really wanted his mother and father to meet Rachel, but that just wasn't in God's will. Later in the day Israel and his camp stopped in Migdal Eder and set up lodging. They stayed in that area a little longer than anticipated and while there one of Leah and Israel's oldest son, Reuben, did something rather unspeakable!!

Reuben had been checking out his father's side chick, Bilhah. Bilhah was Rachel's maid. He had been checkin' for her since he was a little boy. He had a school boy crush on her and now that he was a man he had every intention of being with her. So one night while the camp was asleep, Reuben was creepin' about and slipped his way right into the side chick's tent and bed. He did not rape her, but he did have sex with her or as he called it 'he made love to her.' Jacob heard about what happened the next day but said to himself, "I have too much on my mind and my heart is still torn and grieving for my sweet love Rachel, I just can't deal with this right now."

It seems that out of the twelve son's that Israel had, it was Leah's sons that had heart and boldness. It was two of Leah's sons Simeon and Levi that killed the entire town and now Reuben has slept with is father's side chick. Reuben was Jacob's first born son so he had been watching Bilhah for a long time.

Israel's twelve sons are as follows: Sons by Leah and Jacob are Reuben, Simeon, Levi, Judah, Issachar and Zebulun. Sons by Leah's maid Zilpah are Gad and Asher. Sons by Jacob and Rachel are Joseph and Benjamin and finally sons by Rachel's maid Bilhah are Dan and Naphtali. All of these sons were born in Paddan Aram. Israel had two wives, two side chicks, eleven boys and one girl. Now you see why it is said that Jacob had a BANK of chiren, you cannot count them on one or two hands.

After a very long and tedious journey, one filled with stress and death Israel and his camp finally reached his hometown Mamre in Kiriath Arba or MKA which is now known as Hebron. This is the same place where Abraham and Isaac had also lived before the burning and destruction of Sodom and Gomorrah.

When the town realized that it was Israel and his people horns started blowing and fireworks were going off because Israel had finally returned home. Israel couldn't wait to see his father and mother and show off his family and tell them how good God had been to him. After all of the introductions and hugging Israel sat down with is parents and said, "Mom and dad I want you to know that sending me to live with uncle Laban, although he is a con artist, was one of the best things you could have done for me because it matured me and caused me to have a closer relationship with God. Not to mention that I met my beloved Rachel. I really wish that you could have met her."

Israel's parents did not understand why he was now calling himself Israel when his government name was Jacob, but after Israel explained what happened between him and the angel they were on board and also started calling him Israel.

All of the excitement and the stories that Israel told his parents must have been too much for his 180 year old father, Isaac, because right in the middle of Israel telling how his two sons killed an entire town by themselves to avenge the rape and kidnap of their sister Dinah, Isaac gasped and took his last breath.

Israel was already grieving the loss of his best prayer warrior and Rachel's nurse Deborah, along with grieving his beloved and recently deceased wife Rachel and now to add more sorrow to his plate, his dear old father transitions to heaven right in the middle of their conversation. Israel was overwhelmed with grief. If you have ever wondered where the saying 'Death comes in threes" came from well now you know.

Israel and Esau came together and planned the grandest home going service for their father Isaac. He lay in state at the capitol of MKA for two days and then he was buried with the rest of his family, Abraham and Sarah.

This moment in Israel's life was one that he never thought that he would be able to get past, but as my mother often says, "This too shall pass." And guess what, it always does.

93

Point (s) to Ponder: Why was Jacob and Rachel's prayer regarding what to do answered so quickly and definitely by the Lord but when Rachel was at death's door Jacob's prayer to save her life was not answered? Rachel is the one that stole her father's false idol gods and brought them on their journey and just before they left for Bethel Jacob told all to throw out their idol gods could this have had something to do with Rachel's death? Are the two somehow connected?

Take Away: Be thankful for the time that you have with your loved ones because just like Deborah, Rachel and Isaac suddenly passed away, we all have an expiration date. Don't let your loved ones leave without knowing that you love them and definitely don't let loved ones die without mending broken fences.

Prayer: Father we thank you for those that You have placed in our life whether it is family or friend. We ask that You would give us the heart to show them love and compassion and to always hold them dear in our hearts as You keep us in Your heart.

Ch. #8 – Genesis 36 – Esau and Jacob split like Abram and Lot

In the previous chapter we saw how Jacob (Israel) suffered great loss and he and his children finally reached his hometown MKA. In previous chapters we witnessed Jacob's interesting life story front and center and what had been going on with him over the years but what about Esau? What had Esau been up to in the last 14+ years?

Esau was also called Edom, just as Jacob was called Israel. I guess that it was a twin thing. Now Esau had been a very busy man since Jacob left. His parents had not forbidden him to marry the women of Canaan so Esau had a field day running through the women there. He finally settled down and decided that three wives would be just enough to keep him from runnin' the streets and being a womanizer. Yes, Esau had an appetite for the women.

I guess that after working hard in the field all day and having the constant reminder that his inheritance had been taken from him twice by his little twin brother Jacob, he was looking for love in all the wrong places but he finally found it on a one street. Why did he find it on a one way street and not a two way street, because before he found and married his first wife Esau was nicknamed "One Way", he gained that nickname because it was always all about him, his way or no way, he was quite selfish and self-centered due to being hurt by his mama, twin brother and daddy. Instead of getting counseling to help resolve his issues, he took his frustrations out on the women in the area because the hurt that he felt ultimately spawned from his ear hustlin' mama's sinister scheme.

Esau's first wife was named Adah. She was the daughter of one of the local Hittites named Elon. Adah had a baby boy for Esau and she named him Eliphaz.

Esau's second wife was named Oholibamah (Oh Holy Bama) and she was the daughter of a Hivite named Anah and the granddaughter of the Hivite named Zibeon. Oholibamah had three sons for Esau and named them Jeush, Jalam and Korah.

Esau's third wife was named Basemath and she was Ishmael's daughter, which made her Esau's cousin! Ishamel was the first born son of Abraham and Abraham was Esau's uncle. Yes, another cousin couple! Ishamel's first born son was named Nebioth.

Why is this important because Ishamel wasn't having Esau's womanizing ways put on his daughter! He saw how Esau ran through the women and he and his son Nebioth stepped to Esau and told him, "Look nephew, we see you!! We know how you act out here in these streets! Now you wannna come checkin for your cousin Basemath!! If you come over here you had better come correct or keep it movin'! We will not allow you to take Basemath's cookies, impregnate her and move on like you never knew her. Remember the following words, let them vibrate in your mind and heart - to see her and to have a relationship with her means that YOU WILL MARRY HER!! Do not let us have to come for you!!"

Esau completely understood and said, "I get it! Believe me I do! I will do the right thing for Basemath! My intentions towards my cousin are good! Believe me I will not hurt shawty's heart."

So Esau married Basemath and of course she became pregnant and had a son named Reuel. It was Esau that gave him his name. In the Urban dictionary the name Reuel means a sweet caring person who will never leave your side when you are in need. I am guessing that Esau knew that Basemath's father and brother weren't playing and he wanted them to know beyond a shadow of a doubt the he was that guy!! He wanted them to know that he would be a sweet caring husband who would never leave Basemath's side. Smart man!!

Esau met his three wives in the land of Canaan, his hometown. He married them and had children with them and now he was thinking that since his twin was back on the scene maybe he could spread his wings, start out fresh and get away from so much family and all the history. I understand what Esau was doing because sometimes family just won't let you change and won't recognize that you have changed. They seem to hold onto the past.

Esau and Jacob both had many children and wives as well as a lot of animals and possessions. Just like Abram and Lot their possessions became too much for the land and they were draining the resources at a faster than normal rate. They both had so much and something had to be done.

Esau thought to himself, "I have stayed her all of these years and taken care of mom and dad, now it is time for me to spread my wings a little bit. The land is not enough for me and Jacob so I will be the bigger man and move away. After all he just got back from being away 14 plus years and on top of that he lost his beloved wife Rachel.

He probably needs to be here in his hometown where people know him. Hmm. What I will do is this, I will do him and me a solid and move away."

So Esau gathered up all of his wives, children, animals and possessions and moved away from his brother Jacob. He finally decided to settle way out in the country. Yes, Esau left the city to raise his children in the country of Seir. He felt that they would have more room to roam and play and more importantly not get caught up in what goes on in the big city life.

Once they were living the good country life and Esau's sons grew and matured they began to act like grown men and made Esau a grandfather. Esau's chest and head was so big and he walked around puffed up because he had many grand and great grands. You could tell that they were Esau's children, grandchildren and great grands because they were all hairy, red and a bit on the smelly side. They followed right in Esau's footsteps regardless of how smelly those footsteps might have been.

Remember that Esau had a son named Eliphaz from his wife Adah, well chile this was a busy young man. He had six sons named Teman, Omar, Zepho, gatam and Kenaz. His sixth son was from a side chick named Timna who had a son for Eliphaz named Amalek. These six grandsons became the high ranking head men in charge of the city of Edom.

Reul, Basemath's son, had four sons named Nahath, Zerah, Shammah and Mizzah. These four also became high ranking head men in charge of the city of Edom.

Oholibamah's three sons Jeush, Jalam and Korah became high ranking men in charge at Edom. It seems that Esau made a wise decision to move his family away from the city life. All of his sons were educated, men of influence and had high paying prestigious careers. Remember that Edom is another name for Esau so apparently Esau's family grew so big that the town was named Edom and his sons ran it.

There was a man in the land named Seir who was a Horite. The Horites were cave dwellers. Seir had seven sons who were called the Dukes of Horite. Their names are Lotan, Shobal, Anah, Dishon, Ezer and Dishan. How does this tie in to Esau, well, one of Esau's sons named Eliphaz had a side chick named Timna, and Timna was the granddaughter of Seir and the daughter of Sier's son Lotan!!

Lotan had two sons named Hori and Homan and of course the side chick daughter Timna.

Lotan's brother Shobal had sons named Alvan, Manahath, Ebal, Shepbo and Onam.

Lotan's other brother named Zibeon had two sons named Aiah and Anah. His son Anah was known for being the one who found a hot spring in the wilderness when he was taking his father's donkeys out to graze in the grass. This was a great accomplishment and gained him great notoriety, because now the people could go from the cold damp cave to soak in the hot springs and get relief for their aching bones. Caves were known to be dark, damp and moist and dampness and moisture can have a negative effect on human bones and cause Arthritis, Osteoarthritis, Rheumatoid arthritis and even Lupus, so when I tell you that finding that Hot Spring made him famous among his people, it really did!!

Anah's fame went to his head and caused him to have to one son and a daughter. His son's name was Dishon and his daughter was Esau's wife Oholibamah.

Dishon rode off of his father's coat of fame, learned the business of managing the hot springs and had four sons named Hemdan, Eshban, Ithran and Keran.

Ezer, Lotan's little brother, had three boys named Bilhan, Zaavan and Akan.

The youngest brother of Lotan named Dishan had two sons, Uz and Aran.

So as you can see the seven Dukes of Seir were busy men.

Now besides the seven dukes there were also kings who were over Edom, long before Israel (Jacob) even thought about having a king. Bela, son of Beor, was the first king to rule the city named Dinhabah. When Bela transitioned to be with the Lord Jobab, son of Zerah, who was the son of Simeon, Leah and Jacob's son, was next in the pecking order and became king.

After Jobab passed away the next king up to bat was Hushan who was a Temanite. When Hushan the Temanite passed away Hedad the son of Beda gladly took the kingship. He did not have to run for office or campaign, just like the other kings and the kings to come after him, it was automatic due to bloodline. Hedad was pretty powerful because in his time as king a war broke out with the Midianites in the city of

Avith and Hedad went to war and took them out at the city of Avith. He had a reputation for kickin' butt and not taking names.

When Hedad finally passed Samlah of Masrekah were placed in the kingship position. After Samlah there was Shaul from Rehoboth-on-the-river. When Shaul went onto be with the Lord Baal-Hanan son of Acborb became King. When Baal-Hanan died Hadad of the city of Pau became king and was accompanied by his wife Mehetabel daughter of Matred and Me-Zahab.

Everything listed above simply gives us the full picture of who was who in Edom and as well it gives us the bloodline of Esau.

This chapter right here!! This was worse than going to a family reunion and trying to remember family member names that you never met! However, it does serve its historical purpose.

Point (s) to Ponder: Was Esau really being the bigger man by moving away from his hometown or were there other underlying reasons? Could it be that the more he saw his twin brother Jacob, the more those old feelings of wanting to kill Jacob for taking his inheritance came back or did he just want to spread his wings and get away from the place that he had lived most of his life?

Take Away: Just as Esau's kingly family tree is acknowledged and highlighted in this chapter, let us seek to find what our family line holds. When we do this we honor those that came before us and open the door for future generations to know their past and where they came from.

Prayer: Father we thank You right now for the history of our lives and for the lineage of our bloodline. We ask that our eyes are open to see how precious the lives of our ancestors are because they set the clear path for us to be able to walk in our destiny which is in You.

Ch. 9 – Genesis 37 – Joseph's big balla dreams

Esau and his family had moved away from his hometown and relatives while Jacob (Israel) decided to settle down and stay in his hometown of Canaan. When we take into consideration how quickly Esau hauled butt out of his hometown it does seem that Esau couldn't wait to get away from relatives, be his own man and do things completely his way without interference from his ear hustling mama. Now that his father had passed away and Israel was back to stay, Esau figured that Israel could take care of their mama, especially since Jacob was her favorite son.

What is going on with Israel and his sons? Does Israel have a favorite son out of the dozen sons that he has? Will he be like his mama and be so obvious with his favoritism that it causes family dysfunction? Let's check it out, but first I think that we need to be reminded of who Israel's sons are and who their mothers were.

1) Reuben (Leah)

2) Simeon (Leah)

3) Levi (Leah)

4) Judah (Leah)

5) Dan (Bilhah-Rachel's maid)

6) Naphtali (Bilhah)

7) Gad (Zilpah- Leah's maid)

8) Asher (Zilpah)

9) Issachar (Leah)

10) Zebulun (Leah)

11) Joseph (Rachel)

12) Benjamin (Rachel).

Israel had a bank of chiren, but who is his favorite? Let's go forward and find out!

When Joseph, Israel and Rachel's son and Israel's second to the youngest son was seventeen years young, Israel would have him to go in the fields with his brothers to not only help them herd the animals but to learn all that he could about what his brothers were up to. Were they actually working or were they slackin' and shammin'.

Yes, Joseph was a little nosey irritating daddy's boy. As soon as Joseph got the 411 on what was going down in the field with his brothers he quickly ghosted them and ran off to his father to snitch like he was getting paid to be a confidential informant! Joseph was always getting the others in trouble with their dad.

Israel loved the reports that Joseph gave him on what was going on in the fields and Joseph quickly became Israel's favorite, however just as quickly as he became his father's favorite son, his brothers despised him and couldn't stand the sight of him. None of them would even speak with him and they even looked for any chance to get revenge. "Allegedly" word on the street is that some of his brothers wanted him dead and gone. They were even plotting and scheming!! "Allegedly!"

Joseph only had one full blooded brother, and that was Benjamin, the other 9 brothers were his step brothers or half-brothers. I believe that is why Israel favored Joseph and Benjamin more than the others because they were sons of his beloved Rachel and both of them were born when he and Rachel were in their Golden years! Israel felt that since Rachel had passed away while giving birth to Benjamin, that he had to give them twice as much love, because their mother was gone on to be with the Lord. Israel was so crazy about Joseph that he had a special coat made for him. One that made him stand out as royalty among his brothers. Israel told the tailor, "I want a special long robe made for my favorite son, Joseph. I need you to put your skillz to work because this coat should make him stand out from everyone else and he should look like a person of status and privilege! Money is no object! I want it finely embroidered with many colors, so that it represents God's glory and righteousness that has been placed upon my boy's life!! The BOY is anointed and appointed and I want the world to know!"

Now just how do you think the others sons felt about this? Being pissed off doesn't even describe the level of emotions that they now have towards their father for loving Joseph more than them and even more so towards Joseph for being loved so much more. It's one thing to be your father's favorite, but to actually walk around like you are the king of your siblings and snitching on them, regardless of what they were doing is another! Chile, look a heng, Joseph just didn't know what awaited him.

Now Joseph was not only a little nosey, snitching, thought he was better than everyone else, daddy's boy, but he was also a dreamer. When I tell you that he had destiny dreams that took him far beyond his brothers, buh-leeve me when I tell you that he did. Sometimes we can have elaborate dreams that point us in our direction of destiny, but should we use wisdom before we blast them to everyone else, especially those that will not share the destiny? Let's look ahead and see just what dream blasting did for Joseph.

One day when Joseph and the boys were out in the field and of course Joseph was being observant and taking notes so that he could give his father a thorough "Snitch"report, Joseph decided that he would tell his brothers about the dream he had the previous night. Joseph said, "My brothas, my brothas, I really gotta tell you about this dream that I had last night. All of y'all were in it with me."

His brothers said, "Really!? You had a dream that we were all in? I would have thought that it would only be you and daddy in the dream especially since he made you that fine coat of colors and he has let us know that he loves you more!"

Levi stepped up and said, "Boy, we don't have time for your foolishness today! Did you write this dream in your "Snitch book" and is it only about us? Bruh, miss me with all of that nonsense!"

Joseph said,"Naw man, it ain't even like that! Just like you have a job in the field, my job is to report to daddy what happens in the field. I'm not out to get you, I just gotta do what I gotta do. I can't help it if this burden of reporting has been placed on my shoulders."

Reuben the oldest son spoke up and said, "Burden of reporting. I know that it was you that told daddy that I slept with his side chick Bilhah, right after your mother, Rachel died. Don't play me bruh!"

Simeon said, "We ALL know who you really are and we know that you ain't one of us. So please miss us with that dream mess. We are tired of hearing about your dreams, what about our dreams?"

Joseph said, "Man, y'all got me all wrong! Anyways this is my latest and greatest dream and I know that it came directly from God, why who else would give me such a divine picture of my destiny?!"

All of the brothers said in harmony, "Oh Lord, not again!! Did you just hear us say that we do not want to hear that mess! Keep it to yourself, now we ain't playin' with you!"

Chile, Joseph didn't pay them any attention, none at all!! He kept talking like they never said a word. Joseph continued, "I had this dream where we were all out in the field, much like we are now, and we were all picking up the bundles of wheat…"

This time Judah interrupted, "See, now I know that you are dreaming! YOU picked up a bundle? Ha, ha! The only thing that we have seen you pick up besides your pen and paper is your feet to run and tell daddy what we are doing! Dude, you need to go on somewhere with that bull-harkey mess!!"

Joseph said, "Okay Judah, you got jokes today, ha ha!! Anywho as I was saying before I was so rudely interrupted, we were picking up bundles of wheat and when all of a sudden my bundle of wheat started growing and was so much larger than your bundles and guess what else, your bundles started circling around my big bundle and to top it off your bundles bowed down to my bundle! WOW! I woke up thanking the Lord for showing me my destiny of elevation."

Now if you thought that the brothers didn't like Joseph before you can rest assured that they hated him now!! They all said, "So according to your lame dream, YOU, the family snitch are going to rule over us? We are going to bow down to YOU?"

Simeon stood up and said, "You know what, I just can't with you right now! Dude do you realize who you are talking to? We just slaughtered an entire town of men, robbed banks, jewelry stores and took whatever we wanted and you, you with your scrawny self think that God has told you that you are going to rule over us!! I have the right mind to off your butt right now and be done with you and your dreams."

Joseph thought that he had better be on his way home, because he knew that Simeon had a temper and there was no telling what he was about to do. So Joseph went home and told his father what had happened and about the dream. Israel said, "Son, now while I may believe in your dreams, your brothers may find it hard to believe that you would rule over them, so I would ask you to please only tell me what God shows you."

Joseph heard his father's wise advice but just couldn't control that tongue! Joseph went to sleep and had another dream. He woke up all recharged and ready to go to the fields to tell his brothers. He then remembered that his father told him not to tell the brothers about any more of his dreams, to only tell him. Joseph thought to himself, "It won't hurt for me to tell them just one more, just ONE more. Besides this dream will let them know that I WILL rule over them and they should fall in line now and do what I say to do, that way they will be used to taking orders from me."

So little nosey, snitching, thought he was better than everyone else, daddy's boy, dreamer took his little BE-hind to the field with his brothers and when they took a break he again sat down with them to tell them the dream. As soon as he sat down with them they all looked at each other, shook their heads and gave Joseph the side eye.

Look-a here, if you think that the brother's side eyes made a difference to Joseph and that he would not tell his dream, then you have not been reading and paying attention to this chapter!

Joseph sat down with his brothers and said, "Now I know that after yesterday's dream, you are probably not going to want to hear this one, BUT buh-leeve me when I tell you that you do!! I had another dream last night."

Immediately you could hear the sighs and the moans from the other brothers because they were tired of Joseph and he was workin' their last nerve!   But Joseph did not care he was going to tell them his dream.

Joseph continued, "Y'all need to stop with all of that, I know you don't want to hear this dream, but you NEED to hear this dream. Now as I was saying and back to my dream and puh-leez keep your noises to a minimum! Last night I dreamt that even the sun, the moon and eleven stars bowed down to me!"

At this point Reuben, the oldest brother, had had enough. He grabbed Joseph by the neck and pulled and pinched his ear and they all went to see their father. Reuben pushed Joseph to his father and said, "Daddy, we have had enough of this! This, this, I don't even know what to call him. Yesterday he told us that he had a dream that we

109

would all serve and bow down to him, now today, even though we told him we didn't want to hear it he said that he dreamt that the sun, moon and eleven stars would bow down to him! Who does he think he is, the Messiah?! And why only eleven stars? He is trying to say that all eleven of his brothers would bow to him! He even thinks that you and mom will bow to him!!Daddy you gotta do something with him. Get yo boy! Getcha boy. "

When Israel heard this he went slap off on Joseph. He had never even raised his eyebrows at Joseph before, so this was new and exciting to the brothers, to see special favorite son Joseph get what they always got. In the past no matter what went down, Israel had Joseph's back, but this time even Israel felt that he had gone too far and was doing way too much. Israel said, "I thought that you and I had a talk about this yesterday and I can see that, as usual, you did not listen to me and now you think that you are the Messiah! Who do you think you are? You actually believe those dreams and think that all of us are going to bow down and serve you? I could actually see that you have the potential and abilities to run things, but now is not that time."

When the other brothers heard their father say that he could see that Joseph had the potential and ability to run things they looked at each other, boiling with anger and gave each other the head nod signifying that we must take care of this ourselves. Now we all know that the brothers have a way of scheming and plotting like no other. Poor Joseph just didn't know what was coming his way.

The brothers wanted to get away from Joseph, as far away from him as they could, so they went all the way back to Shechem, the place where they avenged their sister Dinah's rape and kidnap. You know they wanted distance if they went back to that place.

Joseph was looking for the brothers and went and asked his father where they were? Israel said to Joseph, "Good morning son. Getting a late start I see. I guess that is how those in charge that have everyone bowing down to them do things or maybe that is how dreamers do it. Your brothers are in Shechem this morning with the flocks and I need you to go down there. Are you ready to go and check up on them for me?"

Joseph said, "Why of course! The king is ready to check on his subjects."

Israel said, "Now there you go again! Do not go down there talking like that. One of your brothers might take your head off. Go down there and act like you got some kinda sense in your head, find out what's going on and bring me back the report. I don't want to hear about any more of your drama dreams!"

Joseph said, "Ok, ok! I will behave myself, but when I am king I will remember this day."

So with that, Joseph headed out from Hebron to Shechem. Once he was there, he did not see his brothers or the flock but he did see a man and said, "Good morning to you! I am trying to find my brothers have you seen them?"

The man said, "I saw you over there looking all lost and things and I was wondering who or what were you looking for out here in these fields alone. I saw your brothers earlier this morning and heard them say that they were going to Dothan. You do know how to get there, right?"

Joseph said, "Oh yes sir, I know my way around. Thank you for the 411."

Joseph then headed down to Dothan and found his brothers. But before he could get to them they saw him coming! Unknown to Joseph, his brothers had been scheming ever since he had that shady dream about the eleven stars bowing to him. They knew that he was talking about them when he said eleven stars. At least Joseph called them stars, he could have said he saw eleven duds bowing down to him!

The brothers had another one of their sinister schemes in store for Joseph. Poor Joseph he just does not know what's about to go down!

What the brothers were saying is, "Here comes that little nosey, snitching, thinking he is better than us, Messiah, drama dreaming, daddy's boy, shall we kill him and put him in one of these old rain collecting tanks? We can tell daddy that a wild animal came out of nowhere and killed him and by the time we got to him it was too late. I wonder if he saw this in one of his dreams, with his know it all self."

All of the brothers laughed and gave each other the brother man head nod. Reuben, the oldest, heard them and said, "Er uh, ugh, ugh! Ain't no way!! This is not happening and I can't believe that you are actually plotting this! You will NOT kill him, BUT you can throw him into one of the old rain colleting tanks."

Reuben's thoughts was that they could throw Joseph in there and he would come back later, get Joseph out, make him promise not to tell daddy and then send him home. He also felt that being thrown down into one of the old tanks just might give Joseph some time to think about who he really is and to come down off of that cloud he's been riding.

When Joseph finally caught up to his brothers and even before he could get a word out of his dreaming mouth the brothers snatched his little narrow behind up, held him down and ripped that beautiful coat right off of him. None of the brothers said a word, they were bout it bout it! They were on point with getting their plan done! They just grabbed him and threw him in the old rain water collecting tank. Then if that wasn't enough they all rubbed their hands together as if to say 'Well, that's that.'

After the plan came together so nicely and Joseph was out of the way once and for all, the brothers decided to sit down and have a celebration meal. Simeon said as he laughed, "Hey, hey I bet he didn't dream that he would be thrown down into an old tank! Ha-ha! I just love it when a plan comes together and so nicely!"

The other brothers laughed and continued their meal. As they ate they heard something in the distance. They got up and they could see a caravan of Ishmaelites coming back from Gilead. They knew that the Ishmaelites were coming from Gilead because they had several camels filled up with spices, ointments and perfumes. The Ishmaelites were known in Egypt for selling these kind of goods. In that moment Judah said to the other brothers, "Hey! I have an idea. Let's not kill Joseph, after all he is our little brother, what if we sell his old snitchin' dreamin' crack to the Ishmaelites? That way Joseph's blood is not on our hands and we will be rid of him once and for all."

The way that the brothers shouted yes, you would have thought that Judah gave an inside tip on a stock that would make them millions! So, when the caravan was close enough to them, they pulled old Joseph out of the tank and proceeded to sell him.

Since it was Judah's idea he took the lead on this and said, "Good evening gentlemen. We noticed that you are headed to Egypt to sell your good spices, ointments and perfumes and we have something that could bring you even more money, that is if you are interested?"

The Ishmealites and Midianites said, "But of course. When it comes to making money, you are talking our language."

Judah continued and said, "We have a fine young brotha here that is a big dreamer and can talk a good game, meaning he is quick on his feet, so we can let him go for as little as say 30 pieces of silver?"

The Midianites said, "We will give you twenty pieces of silver and not a cent more. After all he is a dreamer and dreamer's tend to stay in their head and not pay attention."

The brothers accepted the offer and with that Joseph was on his way to Egypt. Yes, and of course Joseph tried to talk his brothers out of selling him and he tried to tell the Midianites who he was, but no one was listening, especially since Judah said that Joseph could talk a good game.

Word in the street has it and even the Nightly News Report said that when Reuben went back to the tank to get Joseph out he found it to be empty and he let out a cry and scream that could be heard all the way to Egypt. Reuben thought that the other brothers had killed Joseph and got rid of his body. Reuben tore his clothes in anguish, started walking fast in a circle and hollered out, "Woo-woo-woo! Aww-woo-woo-woo! LAWD, LAWD Joseph is gone! Where is he? What have these knuckle heads done now? What am I going to tell father about his precious favorite son Joseph?"

The brothers were on part three of their plan. They grabbed one of the goats, slaughtered it and took the blood from the goat and put it all over Joseph's beautiful coat. They looked at each other and gave the brotha man nod and proceeded to go to their father to complete the last phase of their plan.

Judah ran into where Israel was and the others followed him. They should have gotten an Oscar for that performance. They were huffing and puffing, one of them managed to let a couple of tears fall and the others were pretending to sob. Judah spoke and said, "Daddy, daddy, look! Oh God!! We found this beautiful coat out there in the woods. We thought that it looked like Joseph's coat, but we wanted to bring it to you to see if it is and to see if you know where Joseph is?"

Israel took the coat and started crying out loud! He said, "Yes, this is my precious son's coat. OMG!! NO!! NO!! Do you think that a wild animal got a hold of him? OMG! I can't imagine what my child must have gone through. How he felt at the hand of the animal. Oh noooooooo!!"

Judah said, "Yes daddy, it looks like the animal must have torn him from limb to limb and ate him."

Israel (Jacob) ripped and tore his clothes to show just how sad he was and how grieved his heart was that his beloved Joseph was gone. The brothers tried to comfort their father, but there was no comfort for him. Jacob's heart was broken beyond repair!

Poor Joseph was chained and handcuffed and made to walk all the way to Egypt. The thoughts running through is mind were fierce. Joseph said, "How could they do this to me, to ME? I am the one that they should bow down to, not sell. I should have listened to my daddy and kept my mouth shut. They just were not ready for what the future holds. I wonder why the Lord did not show me this part in a dream? BUT YOU KNOW WHAT? I trust the Lord and I know that what He has shown me will come to past, this is just a temporary detour to my greatness!! I guess I just gotta encourage myself and hold on to the greatness that God put in me, to get through this."

Once Joseph and the Midianites reached Egypt the Midianites struck a bargain with one of the officials of Pharaoh named Potiphar and Joseph was sold to Potiphar and was put in charge of Potiphar's household affairs. He became Potiphar's personal assistant!

What will become of Jacob? How will his father survive without him?

Point (S) to Ponder: Why was Joseph so eager to tell his brothers about his dreams? Did he simply want to share what he dreamed of or was it to make himself feel better since he had no real relationship with is brothers? Should Israel have been more undercover about showing favoritism to Joseph? Did Israel consider the feelings of his other sons?

Take Away: When God shows us what He has in store for our future, remember to choose wisely who you share it with. Even though people, even family, may act like they are for you, they very well maybe the same ones praying to bring you down. Many do not want to see you succeed and will use all kinds of tactics to bring you down or to keep you down. Choose your circle wisely!

Prayer: Father we thank You today for giving us dreams and visions and for giving us the wisdom to know who we can share it with or if we should share it at all. We ask for knowledge and understanding as we walk out our dreams of destiny.

Ch. 10 - Genesis 38 - Judah dips & he slips, but what about Joseph?

Now that Joseph has been sold to the Midianites things just weren't the same. Israel is in a constant state of depression and grief because his baby boy Joseph was gone and it seems that the guilt has been eating the brothers UP even though they won't admit it. In their hearts they all miss that little nosey, snitchin', thinking he is better than everyone, Messiah, dreaming, daddy's boy!

The thoughts and guilt were weighing in real heavy on Judah's heart. After all he is the one that came up with the plan that lead to Joseph being sold. He often thinks about Joseph and what would have happened if he had not come up with the idea to sell his brother off to the Midianites.

Judah took his portion of the 20 silver pieces that they got for selling Joseph and moved his hind end to Adullam. He ended up living with a man named Hirah whom he had met and became friends with some years ago. While there Judah started checkin' for this beautiful young shorty who was the daughter of a Canaanite man named Shua. Judah was on his game the moment he arrived, because he remembered seeing her when he and his brothers were in town for a night out. Judah asked Hirah, "Hey man, you remember the last time I was here with my brothers and we were all hanging out? Well, I saw this fine young shawty and I have been thinking about her ever since. Do you know where she is? How I can find her?"

Hirah answered, "Yeah man. I remember and I know exactly who you are talking about. She certainly is a fine Nubian queen! Her father's name is Shau and is a Canaanite.

While I do not know her name and it seems that no one does, I can show you where she lives. Bruh, just don't you go over there playin' playa games, cause her daddy don't play that!"

Judah answered, "Thanks man and no I am not here to play playa games. It is time for me to get a wifey, settle down and get down to grown folks business, if you know what I mean."

Hirah took Judah over to Shua's house. Once they were there Hirah told Judah, "Dude you are on your own. I don't want to have anything to do with this, you see if you mess up I still gotta live here, but you can pick up and leave anytime you want! So I'm out! Check ya later."

So Hirah left Judah to handle his own grown man's business. Judah walked up to the door and rang the bell. He saw that fine shawty looking out the window. He put a big smile on his face, bit his bottom lip and bowed his chest. Just as he did that Shau opened the door. Judah stepped back cause Shau was this big cow throwing looking man and the look on his face was like stone. Judah cleared his throat and said, "Er uh, Good afternoon sir, my name is Judah and I am from Hebron. I am one of Israel's sons. I have come to ask you if I could see your beautiful daughter. I also want you to know that I have the sincerest of intentions towards your daughter."

Shau looked at Judah and said, "Yeah, I remember you. You and your 11 brothers were here a few months back acting like wild hoodlums. I heard rumor that you were here looking for my Baby Girl. Have you wondered why she is still single and living in my house? Well, it's because I don't play the radio when it comes to my Baby Girl. Just ask the town's men and they will tell you, if you ain't coming correct and you coming to run a playa game you best keep it movin' cause Shau will hurt you about his Baby Girl."

Judah started sweating and stepped back again but this time Judah dropped to one knee and said, "Sir, I came here with the best of intentions towards your daughter. I haven't been able to stop thinking about her since I saw her a few months ago. I am asking you for your permission to marry your daughter?"

Shau was stunned and stepped back and raised his hands to praise God. Judah didn't know why Shau raised his hands and what he was going to do so he started to run. Shau reached out and grabbed him and said, "No need to run, son! I am thankful that such a fine young man as yourself has come to ask me for my Baby Girl. And yes, you have my permission to marry her."

Judah thought that he would have heard Shau call shawty's real name by now, but her father continued to call her Baby Girl. Shau said, "Baby Girl! Baby Girl! Come on down here. I know that you have been up there ear hustlin' since Judah arrived. Come on down."

Baby Girl came down with a big cheese eatin' red faced smile from blushing and said, "Yes father."

Shau said, "This fine young man has come to my door checkin' for you, BUT he is not like the others, he has asked to marry you and I said yes. Look at what the Lord has done for you!"

Baby Girl was so excited and was ready for the marital relations to begin. She remembered seeing Judah some months ago and wondered if she would ever see him again. Now lo and behold he stands at her front door and waits for her hand in marriage. Baby Girl hugged and kissed her father and thanked him and then she turned and looked at Judah and said, "Hey there with your foy-in self!! I didn't think that I would ever see you again and I have thought about you every day since I saw you. Did you have a wedding date in mind?"

Judah said, "Wow, you are anything but direct, aren't you?"

Shau looked at Judah and cleared his throat, so Judah said, "Well, Yes, how about today! Let's hit the Justice of the Peace at the courthouse and do this thing! Your father and my friend can be our witnesses."

So Judah and Baby Girl (No one ever found out her real name - it is even listed as Baby Girl on the marriage certificate) were married and of course got down to grown folks business!! Before they knew it Baby Girl was pregnant and gave Judah a boy. Judah and Baby Girl named the baby Er. Word on the street is that the baby boy was named Er because that was the first word Judah spoke to Baby Girl's father Shau. Anywho…that's neither here nor there, but after they had Er they decided to move away from Shau and the others and settle down in a town named Kezib, which was in the low lying hills.

Shortly after moving to Kezib, the couple decided to be fruitful and multiply once again. This time Baby Girl had another boy and they named him Shelah. Judah and Baby Girl were a happy couple and loved to entertain and have guests over. They often threw house parties and made quite a living singing and writing songs. It was rumored that Judah had a full blown recording studio and record label with full distribution.

Once their first born son Er grew up Judah wanted to make sure that he had a fine Bae, to keep him settled but the main reason Judah wanted to find Er a beautiful bae is because Judah did not want ugly grand kids. Judah found Er a wife named Tamar, however the relationship did not last long at all! Bruh man down the street said that, "Er did something against the spiritual law of God and that it was even too bad for Bruh man down the street to think about or to speak of! It was so bad that God took Er out. God killed him dead!"

The Live at Five News says that they are in touch with the police detective working the case and will give details as they come in. The investigating detective did say that the police department was calling in a special unit called "SVU – Spiritual Violation Unit" to take the case further because this is their area of expertise. Er must have done something been pretty bad for that unit to be called in and for God to take him right out!

Judah started to ask himself, "Is this punishment for what I did to my brother Joseph?"

Judah had not told Baby Girl about Joseph and what he and his brothers had done. Judah decided to move things forward and did not want Tamar to be alone, so he told his other son Onan, "Son I need you to honor your dead brother Er and take Tamar as your wife."

First of all, where did Onan come from? His birth was never mentioned, but all of a sudden he is on the scene. Seems a bit suspect to me! Secondly, why would Judah want Onan to marry his brother's wife? I guess that those were the customs of old times! Anyways… Onan had one major problem with this marrying his brother's wife stuff! Now, he didn't mind sleeping with Tamar but he didn't want to have children with her because he felt deep down in his spirit that the child would be referred to as Er's son, since that was really Er's wife. Onan just was not on board with that drama.

Onan did honor his brother and his father's wishes and married and slept with Tamar. However, whenever he had sex with Tamar he made sure that none of his semen entered her body. He really did not want to get her pregnant. Onan always made sure that his semen hit the ground rather than Tamar's eggs. Many call it pullin' out.

God did not like this at all. After all God's order of the day was still in affect and that was to be fruitful and multiply, not waste good semen on the ground! So guess what, God took Onan out as well. Yes, God also killed Onan. Thank the Lord that we have mercy and grace today, because God would have a big kill list with that type of drama going on!

Judah was beside himself that he had now lost two sons. He finally came to the conclusion that Tamar should be content as a widow living at her father's house, until his youngest son Shelah grew up.

Now does this really sound like Judah has any intention of letting his youngest and now only son marry Tamar? I think not!! Tamar will be an old lady and his son

Shelah still young and vibrant. Judah thought to himself, "She won't get the chance to kill my only and last son. Not gone happen."

So Tamar moved back home with her father and waited patiently for Shelah to grow up. As time passed and life went on, Judah lost his beloved wife, Baby Girl. She passed away at home surrounded by her loved ones. Details of her death is not known at this time. Judah and Shau and the rest of Baby Girl's family and friends mourned for a month of Sundays!! The home going service was befitting of a princess and had live streamed coverage because Baby Girl and Judah had become music icons.

Once Judah was back on his feet again, he called his friend Hirah and said, "Hey dude, sorry I have been out of touch for a while, but loosing Baby Girl after having lost my two sons was a bit much for me to handle! Dude I felt like I was being punished."

Hirah replied, "Yeah man, I get it! Is there anything that I can do?"

Judah replied, "Well yeah, I need some company. I am going to Timnah to get the sheep sheared. I would normally do it myself but their wool is so thick and long because I haven't touched them since losing Baby Girl, so would you come and go with me? It would be good just to hang out again. The trip is on me. Let's go have some fun! What do ya say?"

So Hirah and Judah went to Timnah and had a great time while they were there getting the sheep sheered. When Tamar heard, from one of her friends that lived next door to Judah, that Judah was gone to Timnah, old girl was on her game. She knew in her heart and deep in her spirit that after Onan died, Judah would not let her marry Shelah.

She felt that and knew that deep in her spirit, and she decided to come up with a master scheme to get her a man! She did not want to be left alone with her father and have the entire town always pitying her because she was a double, 2 time widow.

Chile the rumors were flying and they called Baby Girl "MAN KILLER!" The men said, "Man I wouldn't touch her with a 20 foot pole. Oh no way. Just look at what happened to the Judah's poor two sons. My name won't be in that obituary line up. Not today, not tomorrow, not ever! Miss me with all of that!"

Tamar decided that she would find out where Judah was and pretend to be someone else. Girlfriend took off her big black widow dress and put on some makeup, a lace front highlighted blonde weave, a tight thigh high dress and 6" red bottom heels. She placed a pretty laced veil over her face and found herself a nice comfortable chair in which she sat and waited at Enaim, which was the gate that lead into the city of Timnah.

Lord have mercy!! Chile, when Judah saw Tamar, he did not recognize her and thought that she was a night walking hoe! All kind of chills and thrills were going through Judah's body. He was on a road trip with his friend and wanted to have some fun, so he walked over to Tamar, still didn't recognize her and said, "Hey pretty young thang! Gurl, I see YOU!! How ARE you doing? Wait, wait, don't answer that cause I can see that you are doing just FINE and pleasing to my eyes! The Lord broke the mold on you didn't He?! Would you like to get outta here and have some fun with me? I promise that you won't be disappointed!"

Tamar replied, "I don't know if you have enough money to pay me my worth?"

Judah said, "I can pay you more than these other clowns out here in these Timnah streets. I will send you a baby goat from my flock. How does that sound?"

Tamar said, "I guess it is ok but I would like a little bit more."

Judah said, "Okay, what we talkin'?"

Tamar said, "To be sure that you are a man of your word and not just out here talkin' smack and trickin', I think that you should allow me to hold onto your seal and cord along with your staff until we finish our grown folks business. This way I know that you will pay me, because you will need these back to conduct any type of business."

Of course Judah being "THAT GUY" handed them over, lock, stock and barrel. No questions asked. Look a heng, Judah was ready for some grown folks business.

Tamar took the seal, cord and staff and she and Judah headed out to get a room at a hotel, motel or any kind of inn! Chile, they did not care as long as it had a bed and door for privacy. They ended up at the Timnah Ocean Resort a five star resort that most musicians and stars frequented.

Of course we all know that a few months later old gurl found out that she was pregnant!! She did not say anything to Judah, but rather she went back home, and put her big black widow dress back on and started playing the broken hearted widow role again.

A little later on Judah remembered that he needed to send a baby goat to the street walkin' hoe who had his seal and cord and staff. Once again he asked his friend Hirah to take the baby goat to her. Hirah looked and he looked but could not find her at all, so he went back to Judah and said, "Dude. I have looked everywhere. It seems that she has disappeared in to thin air. Girl gone!"

Judah talked Hirah into trying one more time so Hirah went back out and spoke to a few men that he saw near the gate where Tamar had been sitting, he said, "Hey there, do you remember the street walkin' hoe that used to sit here in this chair, if so, have you seen her?"

The men looked at each other and said, "We have never seen a street walkin hoe around here at any time. Man this ain't the red light district or hookin' row."

So once again Hirah went back to Judah and said, "I have looked all over and even asked a few men, but no one knows of her or has seen her."

Judah said, "Hmmm. I really need my seal, cord and my staff. I guess we both got what we really wanted. I did what I told her I would do and tried to give her the baby goat. I guess I will just have to call the fraud department and report my stuff stolen and order new ones. I won't keep asking around because people will start rumors about us saying that we are sex traffickers or pimps and I do not need that type of drama or publicity."

Time went by, about three or four months to be exact and word from the street came to Judah that Tamar had been out there in them streets acting like a hoe and she is now pregnant!

Well, needless to say, that did not go over so well with Judah, because yelled at the top of his lungs, "Bring that hoe out here and burn her alive! Burn the hoe now!"

The men went to get her and she responded, "Back up Skippy, BACK IT UP! You don't know me! I ain't no hoe!! The man that I am pregnant for is the owner of this seal, this cord and this staff! Find this man and you will find my baby daddy! So go on somewhere now and stop calling me a street walkin' hoe! I done told you, you don't know me and you betta back up off me!"

When the men ran back to Judah and told him what Tamar said Judah ran over to see the items. But on his way there he did however remember that his seal, cord and staff were missing and the timeline added up to Tamar's pregnancy. When Judah got to Tamar house and saw the items he was floored. His mouth literally fell wide open. His friend Hirah said, "Dude, close your mouth. I can see all back up in there. I see your tonsils. Close it up! Please!"

Everything that Judah had done in Timnah with the street walkin' hoe who he now knows is Tamar came flooding back to his memory. Judah said, "OMG!! How could this be? Gurl, what kind of game are you runnin'?"

Tamar said, "Oh, don't act like you don't know how I got these! You know all too well that you handed them to me thinking that I was a prostitute or as you put it a street walkin' hoe. Y'all listen up I am about to give you the 411, the low down and the tea!! Yes, this here fine outstanding community leader, Judah and I went to the Timnah Ocean Resort, he thought that I was a street walkin' hoe, so what does that say about him! When we got to the resort we enjoyed each other's bodies for at least 5-6 weeks straight. Now he wants to act like what? Like you don't remember! I don't think so! Fess up man! Tell the truth and shame the devil - oh I forgot at this moment you are the devil comin' over here to my daddy's house trying to shame me in front of everyone! I don't think so skippy!"

Judah said, "Oh LAWD! What have I done? I slept with my son's wife. I am your baby daddy?! I didn't know that lady was you or I would have never touched you! OMG! Why would you play such a trick and game? Why?"

Judah then looked at the men and said, "It's not her fault at all. I take full responsibility for this. It's all on me, it's my bad. She did this because I would not let her near my son Shelah, let alone talk about marrying him. My other two sons are dead because of her, so I had to protect my one and only son Shelah, so she got back at me by pullin' this."

And with those words Judah never looked at Tamar again and definitely never had sex with her again. He just couldn't think about her in that way anymore.

Nine months of pregnancy came to an end and Tamar's Labor Day was upon her. As it turns out she wasn't only carrying one child, but two. She had twins! The midwife told the whole story and didn't leave out one detail, she said, "Chile, the first baby boy stuck his hand out and I tied a red thread on it so we would know which one truly came out first and then the strangest thing happened, just as I thought he was ready to come out he pulled his hand back into his mother's womb and the other twin came out. I ain't never seen anything like it before in all of my years as a midwife. It was as if the twins were wrestling for first place."

The midwife was not finished with her story she said, "When the brother came out first I shouted OH Lord, he done broke out! And when I said that Tamar named him Perez which means breakout!"

Tamar chimed in and said, "That's the truth right there. That's just how it happened. After what went down with the hand and all, I couldn't name him anything else but Perez, cause my boy BROKE OUT!! Yes he did!"

The midwife agreed and continued, "When the other one came out with the red string tied to his hand, that child was so light bright we thought the sun was shining and it was 10 pm! I mean really light and bright so his mama, Tamar, named him Zerah which means bright. And that's how it all happened."

Tamar shook her head, looked at her two sons and thought to herself, "Did I have two sons to replace the two husbands that I lost? I am very thankful for them and now I won't have to be alone!"

When Judah heard about her having two sons, twins, he ran over to see them and when he looked at them he asked himself the same question, "Are these two boys here to replace my two sons?"

One thing for sure Judah got his wish, he didn't have any ugly grandchildren (at least not in his eyes) because they were the spitting image of him! Didn't look like Tamar had anything to do with it at all. Yes, Judah became "father granddaddy."

With all of that drama happening in Timnah between Judah and Tamar, there was no mention of Joseph, no one heard from him, knew his whereabouts or knew anything about what was happening with him. Judah and the others knew that Joseph was alive, but had no idea of the journey that selling him to the Midianites had put him on. What is really happening with Joseph? Has he had more dreams and has his original dream come true? Stay tuned for Part three of this series to find out whazzup with Joseph and if everyone is taking a knee before him.

131

Point (s) to Ponder: Why did Judah leave the family and his brothers so abruptly? Had he been planning this all along or did the guilt of what he did to his brother drive him away? What did Judah's first son Er do that was so bad that the Lord killed him right away? Why was it so important for Onan to not spill his semen on the ground and why did this anger the Lord so much?

Take Away: Remember that no matter how far a person tries to run from what they have done, it will eventually catch up with them and if it does not directly affect them, it could be punishment that is passed down to their children or grandchildren. Confess your sins one to another (be so wise about who the other is) and God is faithful to forgive you.

Prayer: Father we thank You today that You have not only placed the do right spirit within us, but that You have also given us the ability to do what is right in Your eyes.

www.ingramcontent.com/pod-product-compliance
Lightning Source LLC
Chambersburg PA
CBHW081538040426
42447CB00014B/3410